Dr. Robert Redfern is a qualif
10 years experience of teachin
finance to non-financial adult:
managers. He has first degrees in both Management
and Technology and Mathematics and Information
Technology. He has a Post Graduate Certificate in
Adult and Higher Education and a Masters in
Business Administration. Robert worked as a CEO
for several retail supplying companies before
becoming a university lecturer initially in Retail
Marketing at the University of Central Lancashire
and then he taught Management Accounting and
Financial Accounting to undergraduates and
postgraduates at Manchester Metropolitan
University. He went on to teach the Business Studies
degree course at the Open University Midlands
Region. Robert also has a PhD in Retail Product
Development gained whilst a Research Fellow in the
Department of Art and Design at the University of
Salford.

Of course Robert sells on eBay too!!

Sole Trader Accounting

– A Complete Bookkeeping Training Kit 2

Robert Redfern

UK Tax, 'Single Entry, Cash Basis and Simplified Expenses' Version

LARGER PRINT EDITION

Published by **Robert Redfern**

First published in 2016, Revised May 2019
Copyright © Robert Redfern, 2016

The moral right of Robert Redfern to be identified as the author of this work has been asserted by him in accordance with the Copyright, Designs and Patents Act 1988.

Exclusion of Liability and Disclaimer

NOTE: The material given here does not deal with particular circumstances and is presented in good faith. UK tax laws and accounting regulations are subject to frequent change and are complicated, so readers should carefully check the latest position with the tax authorities or consult qualified advisors before using the book material for their own business bookkeeping. It is impossible to predict all the circumstances in which the book and kit may be used. Accordingly the author and publisher shall not be liable to any person or entity for any damage or loss caused by the information contained in or omitted from this publication.

This book contains web links to free providers of software. Please note that web page addresses can change and you may need to search for the current software yourself.

All rights reserved.

No part of this publication may be reproduced, stored in a retrieval system or transmitted, in any form, or by any means, without the prior permission, in writing, of the publisher, nor be otherwise circulated in any form other than that in which it is published without a similar condition being imposed on the subsequent publisher.

Dedicated to my wife, Jan

CHAPTER ONE – INTRODUCTION – GETTING STARTED	6
CHAPTER TWO – SIMPLE EFFECTIVE BOOKKEEPING	24
CHAPTER THREE – BANK STATEMENTS	43
CHAPTER FOUR – CASE STUDY INTRODUCTION	58
CHAPTER FIVE – SIMPLEX STYLE ANALYSED CASH BOOK	65
CHAPTER SIX – SALES AND PURCHASES BOOKKEEPING	77
CHAPTER SEVEN – LESS TAX – EBAY AND PAYPAL FEES	102
CHAPTER EIGHT – FINALISING CASH BOOK POSTINGS	117
CHAPTER NINE – FILING SYSTEMS	136
CHAPTER TEN – NEW TECHNOLOGY – SPREADSHEETS	149
CHAPTER ELEVEN – A FREE CLOUD BASED SYSTEM	175
CHAPTER TWELVE – COST STRUCTURE AND PROFIT	198
CHAPTER THIRTEEN – TRANSFER TO TAX RETURN	208
CHAPTER FOURTEEN – A PAYPAL STATEMENT	218
CHAPTER FIFTEEN – APPENDIX	223

Chapter One – Introduction – Getting Started

Introduction

Welcome to this bestselling book and optional online extra training kit resources for Sole Traders who want to save money by doing their own bookkeeping and UK tax return.

The system you learn here is very simple since it uses single entry cash basis accounting. This means that there are no debits and credits of double entry bookkeeping and, no balance sheets, no asset registers, no accruals or pre-payments, no trial balances and no sets of ledgers.

Cash basis accounting means that you enter transactions into your records when you pay or get the money for the transaction.

Many of the eBay cheap software packages on a CD or a download are simply charging for the open source free accounting package called Gnu Cash, which does have a good help section if you need to learn about double entry accounting, but for the small trader is far too complex.

If you are thinking about buying a DIY bookkeeping manual check first to see if it involves balance sheets and double entry. These complications are just not necessary for a small business selling less than £85000 a year of goods or services.

This book is quite different, it is simple and easy to learn bookkeeping using a Case Study that you follow and can then later apply to your own small business.

How this book (and extra resources kit) is organised:

Introduction – The rest of this introduction explains why and how this book will help you. The training materials in the book include a set of a Sole Trader's typical Case Study business source records for you to practice bookkeeping and record filing with. Also included at the back of this book are bookkeeping forms to fill in. You can just use these if you wish rather than the emailed materials. But in the emailed files there are extra documents (invoices) and a specially designed Sole Trader bookkeeping spreadsheet and another 'What If?' break-even calculator spreadsheet you can use for your own self-employed business.

Part One – Chapters Two to Nine. What is bookkeeping? Begin your training with a simple bookkeeping exercise, using items from your downloaded kit materials - a bank statement, bookkeeping form and a purchase invoice. Or read along with the demonstrations in this book of all the paperwork and techniques.

You learn about source records and some new simpler UK tax rules that influence the way you 'do the books'.

In the next few chapters, as you extend and complete your bookkeeping practice sessions, you learn more about the Case Study Sole Trader and her business records' bookkeeping.

For 'eBayers' there is a special section on how best to treat PayPal and eBay fees with some money savings tips. We end Part One with a master class in source records filing.

Part Two – Chapter Ten. Having mastered the arts of both bookkeeping and filing with the Case Study source records and bookkeeping forms, it is time to move technology on to using the free bookkeeping spreadsheet that works with free open source spreadsheet software. You learn the benefits of the time saved and the access to instant profit updates.

Part Three – Chapters Eleven to Twelve. Moves the technology on to a Cloud based system, if you are interested, with instruction on the free trial of QuickBooks Self-Employed UK tax version which can connect to your Bank and/or PayPal accounts. This access anywhere, web based, Cloud system can free up more time and use images of source records for filing. You learn how to safely download bank statement files if you prefer not to have a live connection to your bank account. This part also includes demonstration of the provided free kit spreadsheet that works out your own business break-even point and can be modelled to see the impact of different selling prices, costs or sales levels.

Part Four – Chapter Thirteen. Covers the transfer of your bookkeeping totals to your tax return. You only need three figures of total sales, total expenses and profit from your forms, spreadsheet or Cloud based bookkeeping system.

Part Five – Chapters Fourteen to Fifteen. A quick tutorial on downloading your PayPal account statement which needs special treatment and then instructions about how to access the kit extra resource materials. Finally some copies of the book materials so you can read about them on the move.

The book makes bookkeeping easy to learn.

This book also explains how, starting by reading and understanding the lines on a bank statement, you begin to see just what bookkeeping is about and how easy it is for the sole trader.

You are probably wondering how you are going to learn how to 'do the books' when you do not have any 'books' - whatever they are.

As we have explained above, this book provides a comprehensive set of sole trader Case Study materials that include Cash Book forms that use the Simplex style, Sales and Purchase Invoices, PayPal, Bank and Credit Card Statements, Till Receipts and Spreadsheet Worksheets.

Now might be a good time to look at the Appendix to get a feel for these items of bookkeeping training materials.

This would also be a good time, if you wish, to email the author at rgredfern@hotmail.com for the files that enable you to print out all the extra kit training materials and access the kit spreadsheets and Cash Book forms to try out sole trader bookkeeping with. You will need a PC or laptop connected to the web and a printer for this.

But you can just follow everything in this book if you wish.

Once you can follow the Case Study bookkeeping using a pencil and the Simplex style Cash Book forms provided, you can progress, if you wish, to using a dedicated but simple Analysed Cash Book Spreadsheet that runs on a PC or Laptop using free spreadsheet software.

This spreadsheet can also be used later for your own small sole trader business and will save time and tell you what your profit is and provide the figures for your tax return.

We go on to help you try a free trial of a Cloud based computer bookkeeping and tax return report system - once you are assured of the basic bookkeeping methods using forms or a spreadsheet. This is optional of course but may be of interest if you like integrating your business accounts with your bank statement records.

You are also taught how to deal with all your sole trader business paperwork correctly so that you can safely keep the six years of records the tax man/woman demands. And on the subject of tax, we show you how to take the figures from your books to fill in your tax returns.

Better get going. Time is money.

But first just a few comments just to make sure this book is right for you in every way.

Who should use this book?

A self employed UK based sole trader (or partnership) who wants to save money by doing their own bookkeeping, although any sole trader will benefit from this kit.

This book is aimed mainly at the UK sole trader, who is self employed, and uses the home at times for some aspect of their business, to keep and manage goods and services or to work on business dealings.

The book uses the latest set of UK HMRC 'Simplified Expenses' tax rules for the self employed sole trader (or partnership) which reduces the burden of bookkeeping to a minimum.

To use this book you need very few mathematical, financial or computer skills beyond being able to understand a bank statement, follow or do simple sums and enter data into the provided Cash Book forms like the one below. You will learn the basics of bookkeeping and then progress step by step to the point where you can do your books and tax self assessment with confidence.

Payments for Business Stock			
Date or Chq No	To whom paid	Cash Col 9	Cheques, credit and debit cards Col 10

Simplex Style Payments for Business Stock

The first few sections of this book will take you to the point where you can manage without an accountant and do your own books. You will also be able to fill in your sole trader business tax returns.

If you wish you can progress further. You are encouraged to try new things such as using a provided formatted spreadsheet (which is included in the files that you email the author for) or using the link to the free trial UK version of QuickBooks Self-Employed Cloud Bookkeeping – no credit card required!§

You will learn how to import files into the free QuickBooks Self-Employed package.

You can import bank statement file data from either a bank account or PayPal statement or even use direct internet linking to your bank and PayPal Fees account. Moving to these spreadsheets and imports are easy to learn to do and they save you time.

Who should not use this book?

A self employed sole trader who has registered their business as a Limited Company, or who has several employees, or who has substantial assets tied up in the business or who sells on credit. They will need a system that uses double entry bookkeeping. This book is based on single entry bookkeeping.

Why use this book?

This book will save you up to £2000 a year in accountants' fees for sole trader bookkeeping and tax returns. If you do not keep a set of 'books' and source records, from you or an accountant, then you risk HMRC fines. The book also gives you a much better understanding of what makes a business tick from a cost and income point of view since, as you progress, you will form a clearer understanding of your business costs and profit and what affects them. Applying the learning from the book to your own business will enhance your financial focus and management of your business profits.

EBay trading using PayPal has some complications when PayPal and eBay take their fees from you that can cost you money. This book explains clearly and simply how to avoid paying more tax if you sell on eBay.

What will I learn from the book?

The book is a self help interactive guide for 'doing the books' of a sole trader.

It assumes no previous knowledge of accounting or bookkeeping.
You learn through the use of a set of sole trader business documents and bookkeeping templates that are provided both in the book Appendix and available by emailing the author.

Later you can use the same templates to do your own business books. The Case Study bookkeeping templates are also completed for you so you can check your progress.

You will learn how to:

Understand how a self employed sole trader can manage without complex accounts
Use the provided sole trader Case Study documents and bookkeeping templates

Identify the three key types of bookkeeping data that your bank statement holds
Collect, use and correctly file key sole trader business documents for 6 + years
Categorise your sole trader expenses using HMRC 'Simplified Expenses' rules for 'allowable' expenses
Understand simple 'cash basis' accounting
Track money in and out of a business
Use sole trader business source documents with supporting information to fill in your provided Analysed Cash Book forms
Split expenses between personal and business
Understand what PayPal and eBay take from your sales income if you use them
Save money on bank charges using a credit card
Simplify and track car/van and home use costs
Manage your business UK tax return

You then also:

Use a provided spreadsheet template (via the Appendix link) to do your sole trader books more quickly and have instant profit updates.

Learn how to use the QuickBooks Self-Employed Bookkeeping package to easily do your tax return.

Automate your sole trader bookkeeping by importing bank and PayPal account statement files to save time.

Link directly to your bank and PayPal accounts to save even more time.

Use a provided spreadsheet to manipulate a break-even point table and understand key profit making ideas

How to use the book

You should read the sections in order since you are learning sole trader bookkeeping in a step by step approach starting with a simple set of sole trader business documents and Cash Book template forms.

You can of course look ahead to see what is coming and get an overview but the later sections build on the knowledge and practice that you have in the earlier sections so we recommend that you do not start half way through the kit.

You will find references to the Case Study trader's filing system of Lever Arch Files, Folders and Boxes. The full explanation of how to use the source document filing system is in Chapter Nine.

This is a book to read plus extra resources training kit; in which is a set of sole trader bookkeeping practice documentary material downloads to print out and practice sole trader bookkeeping from the files sent to you by request from the author. The kit also comes with a spreadsheet to download and again practice sole trader bookkeeping with later on. You may learn more if you download the training materials from the link in the appendix before you start and use them as you read the book, as you will then be handling actual paper invoices and statements, although they are all shown in the book.

The book is also available in a Kindle eBook and in a smaller font (11 v 14 in this book) paperback version.

Learn by doing

The best way to learn how to do bookkeeping as a sole trader is to follow each sort of bookkeeping item - including Sales Invoices, and the various types of expenses - one by one as they are dealt with in this book.

Once you have followed how to 'post' an expense invoice item into the Cash Book and learnt how to file the source documents, you will see that other expenses are dealt with in a similar way, although they are not all exactly the same so some further explanations are given in the book.

Do not be tempted to think that all expenses are treated in the same way for bookkeeping purposes. The kit works through several types of typical sole trading expenses and trains you to deal with shared costs as well as business income related transactions that involve eBay and PayPal fees expenses if you use them. It also covers allowances and purchases by credit card and how some invoices have split items with different timings and separate HMRC expense categories.

Each of these different types is dealt with in this book and each should be read and, ideally, tried out with the kit materials.

You can also use the book as a reference, when completing your own 'books'. It provides a ready set of explanations to use as a guide when dealing with similar transaction items in your own business.

Disclaimer

The information in this book and kit is provided as information only and not as professional financial advice.

This book author has 10 years experience of teaching accounting and finance to non-financial university students and business managers of all ages but he is not a qualified accountant. The kit is designed to help sole traders with a small uncomplicated business to learn how to complete a Cash Book set of accounts in readiness for filling in their tax return using the HMRC 'Simplified Expenses' system, with 'cash basis' accounting. It is not intended for larger and more complex businesses or Limited Companies who use accrual accounting and double-entry bookkeeping and the author recommends that these businesses obtain professional advice from a qualified accountant.

It is time to get going on DIY bookkeeping. If you are near a computer and printer we suggest that you get ready by first emailing the author to get and print off a full set of the Case Study Materials that are shown in the Appendix.

But what is bookkeeping anyway?

Chapter Two – Simple Effective Bookkeeping

Part One

> **What you will find in this section**
> - ✓ **What is Bookkeeping?**
> - ✓ **Bank Statements**
> - ✓ **Case Study Introduction**
> - ✓ **Simplex Cash Book System**

After we define what bookkeeping is and then you join us in having a short practice at it, we begin the study of bookkeeping through the use of some business documents from a typical sole trader Case Study.

Starting with the Case Study shared personal/business bank statement; we focus on just the business and shared transactions. Shared is where maybe we have a split of sharing the cost for example for a telephone bill where the trader shares a home line with the business. We may ignore totally personal items on the bank statement, but need to know which items they are to eliminate them.

We also find out how to get our supporting documents organised into a good filing system, since the tax man/woman can ask to see up to six years of documents plus the current year.

What is Bookkeeping?

Bookkeeping for a small or large business involves 'keeping an accurate and complete record of the financial transactions of a business'.

Here is an example of a bookkeeping record:

Payments for Business Stock			
Date or Chq No	To whom paid	Cash Col 9	Cheques, credit and debit cards Col 10
25/04/20XX	Spanish Shoes	477 60	

Simplex Style Payments for Business Stock

Cash Books

In this record we can see a bookkeeping entry of a business transaction written in to what is called a Cash Book form.

Cash Books forms come in many formats, shapes and sizes including paper, spreadsheets and computer web pages but this particular format above is based on a hardback Simplex D Cash Book that is very popular with small retailers.

The 'Simplex D Cash Book' is available for about £10 from good stationers or Amazon, and has a page for each week of trading, plus summary pages at the back where each week's total figures are entered; in order to then summarise the figures into quarterly and annual business results, including an annual profit and loss statement and a tax return.

The Simplex style of forms is quite a useful way to start learning how to record bookkeeping transactions and in this kit we provide a set of Simplex style forms for you to try out bookkeeping with. Later we move the technology on and give you a spreadsheet version of a cash book to try and then we move on together to use a Cloud web based system.

So the first element of bookkeeping for the self employed sole trader is some form of cash book in which to record weekly transactions like the one above, which we can see is in a Simplex style form called 'Payments for Business Stock'.

Date, Who and Amount

The transaction in the above cash book form has three important pieces of information that make the record 'accurate'. These are the date of the transaction, who was involved and the amount paid. Every bookkeeping entry into a cash book form always has these three pieces of information that accurately pin down the specific transaction that has taken place, so that it cannot be confused with any other transaction.

You will learn how to obtain this key information in this kit.

Source Records

In order to have a 'complete' record of transactions for our bookkeeping, we need to maintain a set of files of the documents that were involved in the original transactions. These 'source' records are typically Sales Invoices, Purchase Invoices, Bank Credit Card and PayPal Statements, Till Receipts, Cheque stubs, Petty Cash Slips, Bank Deposit slips, and Paying in Book stubs
 The source records will need to be kept in a well organised filing system, which we discuss later, since HMRC the UK tax authority can ask to inspect the last 6 years of records.

HMRC Allowable Expenses – Save Tax

The final piece in the bookkeeping puzzle for the self employed sole trader is to make sure that you can separate your business expenditure from your personal expenditure. This is vital if you are to save tax, since you can claim tax relief on what HMRC call 'allowable expenses'. HMRC have a list of allowable 'Total expenses' seen on the HMRC style of layout of tax form SA103S for the self employed trader below:

Business income – if your annual business turnover was below £85,000

9	Your turnover - the takings, fees, sales or money earned by your business	10.1	Trading income allowance - read notes
£ 33570.00		£ 0.00	
10	Any Other Business Income not included in box 9		
£ 0.00			

Allowable business expenses
If your annual turnover was below £85,000 you may just put your total expenses in box 20, rather than filling in the whole section.

11	Cost of goods bought for resale or goods used	16	Accountancy, legal and other professional fees
£ .00		£ .00	
12	Car, van and travel expenses after private use proportion	17	Interest and bank and credit card financial charges
£ .00		£ .00	
13	Wages, salaries and other staff costs	18	Phone, fax, stationery and other office costs
£ .00		£ .00	
14	Rent, rates, power and insurance costs	19	Other allowable business expenses - client entertaining costs are not an allowable expense
£ .00		£ .00	
15	Repairs and renewals of property and equipment	20	Total allowable expenses - total of boxes 11 to 19
£ .00		£ 24500.00	

Net Profit or Loss

21	Net Profit - if your business income is more than your expenses (if box9+box 10 minus box 20 is positive)	22	Or, net loss - if your expenses exceed your business income (if box 20 minus (box 9 plus box 10) is positive)
£ 9065.00		£ .00	

The list for the self employed sole trader/partnership, which is who this book is for (who are not in the construction industry), boils down to this:

Cost of goods bought for resale or goods used
Commission and merchant services fees
Use of home allowance
Car, van and travel use mileage allowance
Use of home allowance
Accountancy, legal and other professional fees
Advertising, web site costs
Bank and credit card etc. financial charges
Phone, fax, stationery and other office costs
Other allowable business expenses – such as a subscription to a trade journal or sundry items not put elsewhere

This list above includes what are known as 'Simplified Expenses'. You can see that whereas the SA103S form has 'Rent, rates, power and insurance we are replacing that with the simplified expenses home use 'allowance'. The same goes for car, van and travel expenses. Simplified expenses use a mileage rate allowance instead.

Simplified Expenses are an innovation by HMRC to make it easier for self employed traders to complete their bookkeeping. They are simplified because they have 'allowances' for vehicle and home use and so the trader does not have to keep records for actual home costs such as rates, rent, insurance, heating and lighting, etc.

The trader also the does not have to spend time calculating how much space the home office takes as a share of the total space in order to allocate and share the home expenses. An allowance is used instead with a similar allowance system for vehicles.

Commission as you can see is not on the SA103S form but it is part of the explanation of the HMRC SA103F (Full) Form Notes, which has the following explanation for the box 17 'Interest' items on that form.

"Cost of goods bought for resale or goods used. This includes the cost of raw materials, direct costs of producing goods sold, adjustments for opening and closing stock, commissions, and any discounts...".

This means that commission such as merchant services fees such as 'Final Value Fees' from eBay and PayPal merchant services fees will be seen as part of the cost of goods sold. This is an important rule that we discuss in more detail later.

You should also note that with sales income of less than the VAT threshold (£85,000 in 2016) you only fill in the total expenses in box 20 of the tax SA103S form. You still need to keep a record of what you have spent in each category though. Some expenses are 'allowable' and others are not. An example, you will see later, is that QuickBooks Self-Employed App will put any bank or credit card charges over £500 a year into a 'disallowed' box in its SA103 Full tax report. Also if you bought some of your own goods yourself then you are not allowed to claim the cost of the goods as an expense and it should not be on the tax form. We need careful use of 'categories' to avoid problems.

Cash Book Categories

The cash book systems all have a way to separate out business expenditure into these 'allowable' expense categories. This means that when you make a bookkeeping entry or 'posting' there is always a specific category on the cash book form for you to use. So for example a transaction for some printer paper will always be entered into the 'phone, fax, stationery and other office costs' category. You will find that since cash books vary that you may get some sub categories as well, so phone may be sub category on some systems.

Your First Bookkeeping

This book provides cash book forms and spreadsheets for you to both train with and then later to use for your own business, but for now we need some training.

It is time for you to try bookkeeping. You can either follow this first example as you read this book or get the full page forms and documents downloads of cash book form, invoice and bank statement (by request by emailing the author) which will allow you to enter the transaction details into a cash book form yourself.

However you can also just use the blank forms on these pages, or those at the back of the book, and fill them in.

The Simplex Book has weekly pages with space for daily entries and we recommend that you get into the habit of doing your bookkeeping every few days or each week so that you are familiar with the current transactions for your business.

There is no right or wrong order in which to carry out your weekly sole trader bookkeeping routine, but you will need your cash book forms, a copy of your bank statement and any invoices that you have collected this week.

For this first practice for you we will assume that you have got your latest Case Study bank statement, a single invoice from a supplier for some business stock to resell and a cash book form. These are shown below starting with the Bank Statement:

Bank Statement April 20XX

Date	Type	Description	Out (£)	In (£)	Balance	
30-04-20XX	DD	CREDIT CARD COMPANY	72.60		1082.53	Postage paid by credit card
29-04-20XX	DEB	MARKS&SPENCER PLC CD 7(	60.00		1155.13	Groceries
28-04-20XX	CR	PAYPAL TRANSFER		560.00	1215.13	Transfer IN of some PayPal balance
25-04-20XX	DEB	SPANISH SHOES	417.60		655.13	Purchases of stock
22-04-20XX	DEB	SAINSBURY'S S/MKT CD 522	70.23		1072.73	Groceries
22-04-20XX	DEB	SAINSBURYS PETROL CD 522	36.95		1142.96	Petrol BUT - Use car allowance
22-04-20XX	DEB	ALDI CD 5220	13.03		1179.91	Groceries
22-04-20XX	DEB	HEATING GAS BOTTLE	30.00		1192.94	Heating gas - Use home allowance
22-04-20XX	DD	TESCO MOBILE 1234567895	8.70		1222.94	Groceries
22-04-20XX	DEB	ASDA PETROL 4415 CD 7025	24.76		1231.64	Petrol BUT - Use car allowance
21-04-20XX	BGC	SAINSBURY AB950		489.15	1256.40	Sainsburys Pay
18-04-20XX	DEB	E H BOOTH & CO CD 7025	8.99		767.25	Groceries
15-04-20XX	DD	HALIFAX INSURANCE C1234	30.00		776.24	Home Insurance - Use home all'ce
13-04-20XX	DD	SKY DIGITAL 002212345678	58.25		806.24	SKY Subscription
12-04-20XX	DEB	SAINSBURY'S S/MKT CD 522	24.45		864.49	Groceries
12-04-20XX	DEB	LIDL UK CD 7025	3.27		888.94	Groceries
11-04-20XX	DEB	OCADO RETAIL LIMIT CD 52	36.09		892.21	Wine
11-04-20XX	DEB	DVLA VEHICLE TAX CD 7025	145.00		928.30	Use car allowance instead
07-04-20XX	CPT	LNK SPAR - THREE W CD 522	50.00		1073.30	Cash for personal use
05-04-20XX	DEB	STATIONERY SUPPLIES	16.54		1123.30	Printer Paper?
04-04-20XX	PAY	BANK FEE	5.00		1139.84	Bank Fee
01-04-20XX	DD	BT GROUP PLC MR73278384	51.16		1144.84	Split
01-04-20XX	SO	OXFAM	4.00		1196.00	Charity donation

And a Purchase Invoice:

Spanish Shoes **Invoice**

Invoice To: Delivery Address:
Mrs. L. Brown Mrs. L. Brown

Businessshoes Businessshoes
3 St Georges 3 St Georges
Grove Grove Date: 25/04/20XX
Greasby Greasby Customer #: 7804
Wirral Wirral Invoice #: 0420
Merseyside Merseyside Terms: Cash Account
CH46 6DD CH46 6DD
UK UK
Phone Phone
Customer ID Customer ID

Qty	Item No	Description	Unit Price £	Total £
4	P14001/09	Mens Derby Lace Up Black Size 9	29.00	116.00
4	P12001/10	Mens Oxford Lace Up Black Size 10	29.00	116.00
4	P14001/11	Mens Derby Lace Up Black Size 11	29.00	116.00
			Subtotal	348.00
			VAT	69.60
			Total	£ 417.60

Make all cheques payable to Spanishshoes
Thank you for your business!

Spanish Shoes Ltd, Seven Acres Business Park, Woodbridge IP12 4PS, UK

We then use a blank Cash Book form:

Payments for Business Stock			
Date or Chq No	To whom paid	Cash Col 9	Cheques, credit and debit cards Col 10

Simplex Style Payments for Business Stock

The bookkeeping process involves cross checking source record documents and entering accurate transaction details into the correct categories, plus some good filing of the source records documents.

The aim is to enter a transaction into the cash book form into the correct category with the three essential accurate pieces of information of exact date paid, who and precise amount.

You could start with the Purchase Invoice above that came with the goods you bought to resell. You are trying to match up the three pieces of information between the invoice and the bank statement.

Here we can see on the invoice that it was for £417.60 and it was issued on 25/04/20XX from a wholesaler called Spanish Shoes. The bank statement also shows that on 25/04/20XX a debit paid Spanish Shoes £417.60. A match! We will discuss this 'reconciliation' of a bank statement with invoices later in more detail. Note that the invoice also states that the amount due is zero, so the supplier has been paid.

Since we have now got confirmation that our business paid for the stock, and we have the exact date the money went out of the business from our bank statement, we can now enter our bookkeeping record in the cash book form above, repeating the transaction details, in the correct category of expense – cost of goods bought for resale – although Simplex call it 'Payments for Business Stock'.

So now you can go ahead and post your first bookkeeping entry and then your 'books' should look like this:

Payments for Business Stock			
Date or Chq No	To whom paid	Cash Col 9	Cheques, credit and debit cards Col 10
25/04/20XX	Spanish Shoes	477 60	

Simplex Style Payments for Business Stock

Well done!

That is how bookkeeping works.

The rest of this book and kit shows you how to carry on posting the rest of the Case Study transactions into your 'books' and also how to file and annotate the source record documents. Filing is in its own section in Chapter Nine.

Payments Other than for (Business) Stock

Having mastered a bookkeeping entry for some business stock we are now going to turn our attention to some of the other typical expenses of a self employed sole trader beyond buying stock.

Apart from purchases, the sole trader usually has these other expenses:
Postage
Packaging
Stationery
eBay listing fees if you sell on eBay
eBay 'final value fees' if you sell on eBay
PayPal fees if you get paid by PayPal
Broadband Contract
Telephone Line Rental
Telephone Call Charges
Bank current account fees
Home use allowance
Vehicle use allowance

We will be using a new Simplex style cash book form, called 'Payments other than for Stock' shown below:

Simplex Book Page Weekly Layout Style
Last Week in May 20XX

Payments other than for Stock		
Nature of Payment	Cash Col 11	Cheques, credit and debit cards Col 12
Employment Cost (i) Wages		
(ii) Inland Revenue PAYE &NI		
Premises Cost (i) Rent and Rates		
(ii) Light, Heat and Insurance		
(iii) Cleaning		
Repairs		
Gen.Admin. (i) Telephone		
(ii) Postage		
(iii) Stationery, etc.		
Motor Expenses (i) Fuel		
(ii) Servicing & Repairs, etc		
Travel & Subsistence		
Advertising & Entertainment		
Legal and Professional		
Interest Payable *PayPal and bank fees*		
Other Expenses		
Lottery Prizes Paid		
Scratch Cards Prizes Paid		
Ebay Final Value Fees		
Car Mileage Allowance		
Working from home allowance		
Totals		

Now this Simplex style of form is not quite designed for the use of HMRC 'Simplified Expenses' so we will have to make some alterations, as you can see, of adding the Car and Home allowances as some extra categories. Simplex has some blank lines for this on every form. We have also added some Ebay, Paypal and Bank fees. We will be <u>not</u> then be using the motor expenses or premises costs in this cash book form and entertainment is no longer an allowable expense these days.

We have separated out Bank fees from Interest Payable since the latter is one that needs special care to avoid paying extra tax if you are an eBay trader and we discuss why in detail later on.

Chapter Three – Bookkeeping and Bank Statements

One of the key source records that traders often start their bookkeeping routine with is a bank statement. The reason for this is that you cannot really enter a transaction into your books if it has not been paid. The source record that shows that a transaction, especially for purchases, has now been paid is the bank statement. We will cover customer PayPal payments IN to your business later.
So a bank statement is a good place to start looking for payment dates, who was paid and the amount.

Bank Statements

Date	Transaction	In (£)	Out (£)	Balance
1 June XX	Starting balance			1010.00
2 June XX	Telephone Company		-45.00	965.00
3 June XX	Postal Company		-19.80	945.20
3 June XX	Wholesaler		-417.60	527.60
5 June XX	Customer Twenty One	74.60		602.20
5 June XX	Customer Sixteen Refund		-72.60	529.60

1. Date   2. Who got paid   3. Amount

First - the date of the transaction.

Second - who got the money — — a supplier or your business.

Third – how much the amount of money was.
 As we suggested in our first try at bookkeeping we are interested in these three pieces of data.

The only tricky bit of those three is if you got money in or was it business money out? However, most bank statements have headings on the columns that say in or out. You usually know if a customer has paid you or if you have paid the telephone bill for the business.

Whilst in and out money affects the balance of the money belonging to the business, a bank statement only tells you who the money went to and not what sort of item or service it was for. We need some supporting source record information for that.

 We need this little bit of extra information for the tax man/woman to make sure an item on the bank statement was for the business or not and so we need to find out exactly what the payment was for.

Not only do we need that bit of extra supporting source document information (on top of the bank statement information) about what the money was paid for, but we also need to keep a set of filed source documentation showing the precise details. We need a filing system too so that if HMRC come and want to check, as they often do, if an item we paid was for the business, we can get our files out and find the relevant source document to prove it was for the business.

Filing is covered in Chapter Nine.

An example of an extra supporting source record document – beyond a bank statement - would be a post office till receipt showing that you paid for an item or items to be posted to a customer or customers for the same amount as on the line of the bank statement for the same date as on the bank statement. The till receipt source document makes it absolutely clear that the money out was 'wholly and exclusively' for business use. The till receipt shows that you spent the money on postage for a customer item and not on a premium bond for yourself for example.

Cash Book Analysis

The final piece of the bookkeeping puzzle as we discussed earlier is to categorise the money in and out into types.
Postage is a type or category of spending. So you must then enter money spent on postage in the 'postage or office supplies' category section of your Cash Book. You will learn exactly how to do this later in this kit. Have a look in the Appendix at the way a cash book layout is organised into these categories in the three forms.

Apart from postage, some other expense categories are: purchases of stock, and telephone costs as in this next example of several bookkeeping 'Cash Book' entries that build on the simple set of bank account figures above.

You can see that now, in our bank statement, the postage and other items have been categorised in a very simple Cash Book type of analysis with several columns in the format below.

Date	Transaction	Revenues	Telephone	Postage	Stock Purchase	Balance
1 June	Starting balance					1010.00
2 June	Telephone April		-45.00			965.00
3 June	Postage purchased			-19.80		945.20
3 June	Inventory purchased				-417.60	527.60
5 June	Product sales	74.60				602.20
5 June	Customer refund paid	-72.60				529.60

Bank Statement items put into CATEGORIES

Accountants call this type of categorisation record of money in and out of the business on particular dates in the tax year an Analysed Cash Book. However the cash book does not have the balance column of a bank statement)

Cash Book is a name and not just concerned with cash. It includes payment by bank transfer, cheque and debit or credit card.

So we can see that the Analysed Cash Book format is like a bank statement but with some extra information that helps us to categorise the money spent into the type of expense category that has been involved in each movement of money or transaction. We get the extra information that is not contained on our bank statement from the source documents that we keep related to everyday transactions.

There are various types of supporting source documents.

As we have said, for postage spending, we get a till receipt from the post office whenever we pay them for the postage cost for an item to be delivered by the postal service to a customer. We would also get an invoice from a supplier of goods that we resell, although if you buy from car boot sales you will have to make a record of your own. This is covered later in Chapter Six.

Another example of a supporting payment document is where we get an invoice from eBay for their fees if we sell on eBay. PayPal on the other hand do not do invoices but give you access to a statement.

We have to file away all these source documents receipts, invoices and statements as proof for the tax man/woman that we spent the money on business costs if he ever wants to see them – and he often does!

And then if you keep using these categories as you record weekly spending in your Cash Book you then know for example how much the business spends on postage over a month or a year. With postage an allowable expense for income tax purposes the amount spent on postage for the business in the year is the amount that your tax bill reduces by. This reduction of taxes applies to all allowable expenses.

So that is what bookkeeping is about. Money in and out, when and what for, and saving tax by using the right 'allowable' expense categories.

More Bookkeeping Practice

Time for you to do some more bookkeeping with another category!

We will examine a business transaction on a much bigger bank statement – one from our sole trader Case Study. This time we can find a stationery purchase which shows up on 05/04/20XX for £16.54 on our shared personal/business bank statement below.

As we have said you need to use an existing document that records the business transaction – such as a bank statement and then have somewhere to record the transaction details again yourself in your 'books', using a Cash Book form with a category of stationery on it.

First examine a copy of these three documents below. You can also print them off when you request the files from the author.

Can you find the supporting evidence to show that the money out for stationery according to the bank statement was for a business expense?
1. Bank statement - joint personal/business. This is a 'source' document where the business transaction has been recorded.
2. Stationery Invoice – a supporting source document that shows what the transaction was for.
3. Simplex Style Analysed Cash Book Form - Payments Other than for Stock section. A form like this is used for each week's worth of transactions, being filled in as you go along. This is part of your 'books'.

Remember we are interested in matching the Date, Who was paid and Amount. Let us examine the bank statement for a transaction that matches the stationery invoice date and amount.

Bank Statement April 20XX

Date	Type	Description	Out (£)	In (£)	Balance	
30-04-20XX	DD	CREDIT CARD COMPANY	72.60		1082.53	Postage paid by credit card
29-04-20XX	DEB	MARKS&SPENCER PLC CD 7(	60.00		1155.13	Groceries
28-04-20XX	CR	PAYPAL TRANSFER		560.00	1215.13	Transfer IN of some PayPal balance
25-04-20XX	DEB	SPANISH SHOES	417.60		655.13	Purchases of stock
22-04-20XX	DEB	SAINSBURY'S S/MKT CD 522	70.23		1072.73	Groceries
22-04-20XX	DEB	SAINSBURYS PETROL CD 522	36.95		1142.96	Petrol BUT - Use car allowance
22-04-20XX	DEB	ALDI CD 5220	13.03		1179.91	Groceries
22-04-20XX	DEB	HEATING GAS BOTTLE	30.00		1192.94	Heating gas - Use home allowance
22-04-20XX	DD	TESCO MOBILE 1234567895	8.70		1222.94	Groceries
22-04-20XX	DEB	ASDA PETROL 4415 CD 7025	24.76		1231.64	Petrol BUT - Use car allowance
21-04-20XX	BGC	SAINSBURY AB950		489.15	1256.40	Sainsburys Pay
18-04-20XX	DEB	E H BOOTH & CO CD 7025	8.99		767.25	Groceries
15-04-20XX	DD	HALIFAX INSURANCE C1234	30.00		776.24	Home Insurance - Use home all'ce
13-04-20XX	DD	SKY DIGITAL 002212345678	58.25		806.24	SKY Subscription
12-04-20XX	DEB	SAINSBURY'S S/MKT CD 522	24.45		864.49	Groceries
12-04-20XX	DEB	LIDL UK CD 7025	3.27		888.94	Groceries
11-04-20XX	DEB	OCADO RETAIL LIMIT CD 52:	36.09		892.21	Wine
11-04-20XX	DEB	DVLA VEHICLE TAX CD 7025	145.00		928.30	Use car allowance instead
07-04-20XX	CPT	LNK SPAR - THREE W CD 522	50.00		1073.30	Cash for personal use
05-04-20XX	DEB	STATIONERY SUPPLIES	16.54		1123.30	Printer Paper?
04-04-20XX	PAY	BANK FEE	5.00		1139.84	Bank Fee
01-04-20XX	DD	BT GROUP PLC MR73278384	51.16		1144.84	Split
01-04-20XX	SO	OXFAM	4.00		1196.00	Charity donation

Bank Statement above and Stationery Invoice below:

Stationery Supplies Co
Invoice for
Your order of 05 April, 2| Order ID 202-0661704-3052340   Invoice number DYTMSDRGb
Invoice date 05 April, 20XX
Qty. Item   Our Pric VAT Rat Total Price
       (excl. VAT)
                    1 5 Star Office Value Copier Paper   20%   £16.54
Wrapped 75gsm A4 White - 1 box containing 5 Reams of 500 sheets
Office Product. B000I6QZNM : 5018206085030
Shipping charges   £0.00   £0.00

Subtotal (excl. VAT)	Subtotal (excl. VAT)	VAT at	Total VAT	Total
0%	20%	20%	£2.76	£16.54
£0.00	£13.78	£2.76		

Conversion rate - £1.00 : EUR 1,29
This shipment completes your order which has been paid
Balance to Pay   £0.00

Simplex Book Page Weekly Layout Style
Last Week in May 20XX

Payments other than for Stock			
Nature of Payment		Cash Col 11	Cheques, credit and debit cards Col 12
Employment Cost	(i) Wages		
	(ii) Inland Revenue PAYE &NI		
Premises Cost	(i) Rent and Rates		
	(ii) Light, Heat and Insurance		
	(iii) Cleaning		
Repairs			
Gen.Admin.	(i) Telephone		
	(ii) Postage		
	(iii) Stationery, etc.		
Motor Expenses	(i) Fuel		
	(ii) Servicing & Repairs, etc		
Travel & Subsistence			
Advertising & Entertainment			
Legal and Professional			
Interest Payable *PayPal and bank fees*			
Other Expenses			
Lottery Prizes Paid			
Scratch Cards Prizes Paid			
Ebay Final Value Fees			
Car Mileage Allowance			
Working from home allowance			
	Totals		

Cash Book Bookkeeping Form Above

How did you get on? Did you find a matching set of a source document and a bank statement entry? Did the date, supplier and the amount on the source document all match up with the bank statement line?

If so then you can make an entry in your Cash Book form 'books'.

The item is not business stock so we need the 'Payments other than for Stock' Cash Book form shown above. Write the amount of £16.54 in the Gen/Admin. (iii) Stationery, etc. line in Cash, Col(umn) 11.

Otherwise you can imagine that you are writing in or 'posting' the stationery item amount into that Bookkeeping form above in the correct category. You are 'doing the books'.

Payments other than for Stock		
Nature of Payment	Cash Col 11	Cheques, credit and debit cards Col 12
Employment Cost (i) Wages		
(ii) Inland Revenue PAYE &NI		
Premises Cost (i) Rent and Rates		
(ii) Light, Heat and Insurance		
(iii) Cleaning		
Repairs		
Gen.Admin. (i) Telephone		
(ii) Postage		
(iii) Stationery, etc.	16	54
Motor Expenses (i) Fuel		
(ii) Servicing & Repairs, etc		
Travel & Subsistence		
Advertising & Entertainment		
Legal and Professional		
Interest Payable		

All that now remains is for you to write "Paid" on the stationery invoice plus the date paid of 05/04/20XX (filing is covered later) and for you to tick off the stationery line on the bank statement. Or imagine you are doing it if you have not filled in the form or printed out the kit materials .

Well done! Your second try at bookkeeping using 'single entry' accounting. It does not get much more complicated than the posting you just did. No debits and credits in two ledgers for you.

A self employed sole trader running a business from home, with few expensive business assets, can use the Cash Book idea of single entry bookkeeping and accounting. This makes it really easy to organise the business audit trail documentary source paperwork and the entries of money in and out of the business into the Cash Book without complex accounting ledgers and a double entry bookkeeping system.

Keeping books like the Cash Book and filed documentary records for your business are your responsibilities to the UK tax authorities (HMRC) if you run a sole trader business.

Cash Book analysis, of money in and out, that looks like an extended bank statement is called 'single entry accounting' which is suitable for small sole traders who do not need the complications of full bookkeeping ledgers that deal with 'double entry accounting' which a larger Limited Company might have. Sole traders are also allowed to have a mixed personal and business bank account.

Single Entry Cash Basis Accounting

Single entry accounting and bookkeeping can also be used with what is called 'cash basis' accounting which is where the transactions involving money in and out of the business are always considered to have taken place on the specific date that the money moved in or out of the business according to the bank statement or PayPal statement.

A larger business or one that is a limited company will use the more complex 'accrual basis' accounting where you charge the accounts with the benefit of goods or services before you may have paid off the bill.

The cash basis idea of specific payment dates reminds us that sole trader bookkeeping is based on bank statements that show the exact date the money left (or came in to) the bank account. But we also need the proof of what the payment was for contained in related source documents that give the extra details - about what the money was for - so that the correct categorisation can take place.

You may know that HMRC do not actually need all this information about categories on your tax return. However you still need to do the recording of expenses into clear categories and keep the paperwork that supports that since you have to show that only 'allowable' expenses are being claimed. If you make no effort to categorise expenses then you cannot show HMRC that the expenses are all in an allowable category and cannot claim to pay less tax.

Summary

This section has explained that 'doing the books' for a self employed sole trader is simply an extension of understanding your bank statement. You then add some information from supporting source documents to pin down expenses into the categories that HMRC have as 'allowable' expenses.

You tried some more real bookkeeping! In the next section we are going to examine some business records from a Case Study of a sole trader who, like you, wants to do her own books.

Chapter Four – Case Study Introduction

Louise Brown – Sole Trader

Louise Brown is a part time self-employed sole trader who works from home and has started (in late March 20XX) selling high quality mens formal shoes using the eBay Buy It Now listings. Her business name for tax purposes is 'Louise Brown trading as BusinessShoes', but she just calls it BusinessShoes.

She spends about 50 hours each month running the business from a spare bedroom in her house in the North of England.
Her business has been up and running for a few weeks, since it started as a hobby selling just to a few friends for no profit.

She has sold 46 pairs so far, with 12 sold in the last week in March and 34 pairs in the three weeks of April so far. She has a part time job too at Sainsbury's.

She buys the shoes from a wholesaler for about £35 including delivery, for each pair in only two colours - black and brown - and in a limited range of sizes from 9 to 11. Louise does not have any extension of credit facilities with the wholesaler yet since she is a new trader.

She therefore pays for these shoes for her business stock in advance using bank transfer. Louise bought some initial stock and now buys about 12 pairs a week and just uses her personal bank current account to run the business rather than have the extra cost of a business account. She has opted for a bank account that she can access via the Internet at any time to check money in and out. She gets paid for all her eBay auction Buy It Now shoe sales through PayPal and she can examine her PayPal account via the Internet as well.

Once the wholesaler has the money for the order the shoes are couriered to Louise's home and they arrive with a purchase invoice which Louise files in a folder along with other business paperwork, bills, receipts, eBay invoices, PayPal and bank account statement updates she prints off every week.

She has decided to use a business subscription to eBay that is the 'Basic' version. This costs about £20 (2016) a month, but does allow up to 200 eBay listings each month without additional listing fees per item. The shoes all sell for about £75 a pair, and this includes free postage for the customer, but Louise must pay the postage costs and account for that expense in her books.

Once a pair of shoes is sold, and they are paid for by the customer using PayPal, Louise gets an email from eBay and can also see when this has happened on her on line eBay and PayPal accounts.
She then parcels up the shoes she has sold and includes a printout of a sales invoice that she produces on her computer. She keeps a copy of each sales invoice for her weekly records folder as well and then she also prints out an address label.

Every time she sells a pair of shoes she takes the items she has sold to the post office and posts them using a small parcel next day signed for postage. Louise drives the 6 miles, there and back, to the post office each day, when items need posting, in her own car.

She has just arranged a new personal credit card which she has started to use ONLY for the postage payments.

This is to avoid too many payments for postage every week showing up in her bank account as 40 to 50 transactions per month perhaps alerting her bank to asking her to have a business bank current account with a monthly fee. Louise can now just have one payment per month of her credit card bill instead on her bank statement. She has set up the credit card direct debit to automatically pay off the full balance every month from her personal bank current account that she now shares with the business.

If Louise sold small lower value items, that did not need to have a 'signed for' acceptance by the local post office, she could use the very useful eBay system that prints a prepaid postage label. Then she could just put them in a post box. The invoice that eBay prints DOES NOT CONFORM to the UK legal rules, so she prints her own, which do have the right amount of information. We list this information in the next chapter.

Louise has a laptop computer she uses to list the items on eBay, which is connected to broadband through her home telephone line. She uses a printer connected to the laptop to print out the sales invoices and every few months she buys printer ink, printer plain paper, wrapping paper and string and parcel tape from an on line stationers. She pays for these items with her shared personal/business bank debit card.

Louise uses the spare bedroom at home for her part time self-employed web trading business and she has a Weekly Document Folder and a set of Lever Arch and Box files where she collects and organises her business paperwork.

The files are marked Purchase Invoices 20XX Lever Arch File, Sales Invoices 20XX Lever Arch File and Box File 20XX to 20XX+1.

Both Lever Arch Files have a cardboard divider to separate UNPAID from PAID invoices. She has some Cash Book Simplex style blank forms - available via the Appendix Link.

Louise plans to do her own business books and self-assessment tax return and save herself accountant's fees, money which she feels will be better spent developing and improving her business.
She is going to try out various the various bookkeeping systems in this book to see what the advantages and disadvantages are of each method.

Case Study Bank Statement

We have already suggested in this book that 'doing the books' for a self-employed sole trader like Louise is easy if you use a 'cash basis accounting' and a 'single entry' Cash Book system, since this means that the bank statement is the basis for it, with some additional information from business source documents related to transactions of money coming in or going out of the business.

Timing of bank statements and entries into the Cash Book

When should Louise enter information into her Cash Book? Luckily for the small trader who is using cash accounting, she does not have to worry so much about the exact timing of her entries. HMRC are not going to care if she enters each business sale every day as she goes along or if she waits until the end of the month when she gets a bank or PayPal statement.

The important date is the one she records in the Cash Book of when money left the business according to the bank statement or came into the business according to the PayPal account statement. In any case Louise can look at her bank statement at any time on the Internet and print out a copy it. What matters is that she can show, through the supporting documents, which her books reflect the money coming in and going out of the business. Louise is learning bookkeeping by trying out a simple system first and then moving her technology on gradually until she will be ready to use a Cloud based system such as QuickBooks Self-Employed. She will use these systems:

- Simplex style Weekly Cash Book
- Analysed Cash Book Spreadsheet
- Cloud Based Computer/Tablet/Smart phone system

Chapter Five – Simplex Style Analysed Cash Book

The Simplex D Account Book Style of Layout

Doing the books used to be just that - a set of books that were ledgers. Although bookkeeping has been computerised and can now be carried out on spreadsheets or using dedicated software, it is quite useful to see how a small self-employed trader like Louise can use the same style of forms as those from a physical Cash Book for her accounts first since it shows us how the basic bookkeeping ideas work.

We can move our technology on, step by step, once we understand what is going on using entries on a piece of paper (a Simplex style of template) as a basis for our understanding.

You have already seen some of the Simplex Cash Book forms like this one:

Simplex Book Page Weekly Layout Style
Last Week in May 20XX

Payments other than for Stock		
Nature of Payment	Cash Col 11	Cheques, credit and debit cards Col 12
Employment Cost (i) Wages		
(ii) Inland Revenue PAYE &NI		
Premises Cost (i) Rent and Rates		
(ii) Light, Heat and Insurance		
(iii) Cleaning		
Repairs		
Gen.Admin. (i) Telephone		
(ii) Postage		
(iii) Stationery, etc.		
Motor Expenses (i) Fuel		
(ii) Servicing & Repairs, etc		
Travel & Subsistence		
Advertising & Entertainment		
Legal and Professional		
Interest Payable *PayPal and bank fees*		
Other Expenses		
Lottery Prizes Paid		
Scratch Cards Prizes Paid		
Ebay Final Value Fees		
Car Mileage Allowance		
Working from home allowance		
Totals		

Look in the Appendix to see the set of larger Simplex style Cash Book forms we are going to use in this book or to get a link to print copies off to try out. Or just pencil in on these pages with forms on them.

We mentioned before that a Simplex D Account Book is a hardback Cash Book that you can obtain from most high street quality stationers or from Amazon for about £10-£12. This is cheap for a year of bookkeeping with a page for each week, expense categories and summary pages, but you have to do your own adding up. The week page is set out as a series of forms (see below) each dealing with a different class of income and expenses. You can see there are forms for payments for stock, non stock and income or receipts.

	Receipt					Paid to Bank		
Date	Takings		Other Receipts	Particulars of Other Receipts	Other Takings	Cash	Cheques	Credit Cards & Debit Cards
	Cash	Cheques, Credit & Debit Cards						
	Col 1	Col 2	Col 3		Col 4	Col 5	Col 6	Col 7
Sub Total	0.00	0.00	0.00	Totals	0.00	0.00	0.00	0.00
Mthly Takings (col 1+2)		0.00						

Payments for Business Stock				Payments other
Date or Chq No	To Whom Paid	Cash	Chq, Credit & Debit Cards	Nature of Payment
		Col 9	Col 10	
				Employment Cost (i) Wages
				(ii) HMRC PAYE/
				Premises Cost (i) Rent & Rates
				(ii) Light, Heat, Ir
				(iii) Cleaning
				Repairs
				Gen Admin (i) Telephone
				(ii) Postage
				(iii) Stationary, e
				Motor Expenses (i) Fuel
				(ii) Servicing &
				Travel & Subsistence
				Advertising & Entertainment
				Legal and Professional
				Interest Payable
				Other Expenses
				Drawings of Partner
	Totals	0.00	0.00	Capital Items (i)
			0.00	(ii)
	Total Payment (to Summary)		0.00	

The Simplex Cash Book originally helped small high street retailers who dealt with cash and paid it into their business bank account every day or so. The Simplex book therefore also has further weekly page sections designed to keep track of the business bank balance until the monthly bank statement arrived.

The Simplex book weekly page layout has sections for Receipts – money in every day, Payments for Business Stock, Payments Other than for Stock, Paid to Bank, Weekly Bank Report and Weekly Cash Report.

We are only going to use the Receipts, Payments for Business Stock and Payments Other than for Stock forms.

We are not using the Paid to Bank, Weekly Bank Report or Weekly Cash Report forms for a number of reasons:

We do not recommend the expense of a separate business bank account as they are unnecessary and an extra expense for the self employed sole trader.

Our bank balance will be shared with our personal expenses and so the bank balance and the business weekly balance will not match.

When we trade via PayPal the money goes into a PayPal account and not our shared personal/business current account.

Gross 'money in' to our PayPal account has automatic deductions from it for eBay and PayPal fees and so the PayPal account balance will not match the Gross income from Receipts.

PayPal also insist that you link your PayPal account to a personal account so that you can pay the fees if you have no money left in your PayPal account.

This makes the bank balance related forms in a Simplex Book of no use to us. However not using some of the Simplex style forms in no way affects our ability to complete our books and submit our tax return.
 Technology has also moved on to eBay, PayPal and Internet banking where we can look at our bank account any time of day or night.

 As a sole trader there is no real separation or distinction between our money and business money as there would be if we ran a Limited Company.

This does not mean that we will ignore our bank balances and the balance of our PayPal account at all. However with a joint personal/business bank account the weekly Simplex bank report form balance tells us little about the state of our weekly shared personal/business bank account cash balance.

Wholly and Exclusively Business

We will follow Louise as she enters into her books a week of expenses and sales at the end of a month and writes up the entries into a Cash Book single entry bookkeeping system.

HMRC only allow you to claim tax relief on expenses that are 'wholly and exclusively for business purposes' so it is important that personal costs are identified and excluded from the bookkeeping process, so Louise must vet her bank statement for her personal spending.

First she will examine her joint personal/business bank statement for the month and start to tie up the lines of the statement with some specific business purchases or income.

Bank Statement April 20XX

Date	Type	Description	Out (£)	In (£)	Balance	
30-04-20XX	DD	CREDIT CARD COMPANY	72.60		1082.53	*Postage paid by credit card*
29-04-20XX	DEB	MARKS&SPENCER PLC CD 7(	60.00		1155.13	*Groceries*
28-04-20XX	CR	PAYPAL TRANSFER		560.00	1215.13	*Transfer IN of some PayPal balance*
25-04-20XX	DEB	SPANISH SHOES	417.60		655.13	*Purchases of stock*
22-04-20XX	DEB	SAINSBURY'S S/MKT CD 522	70.23		1072.73	*Groceries*
22-04-20XX	DEB	SAINSBURYS PETROL CD 522	36.95		1142.96	*Petrol BUT – Use car allowance*
22-04-20XX	DEB	ALDI CD 5220	13.03		1179.91	*Groceries*
22-04-20XX	DEB	HEATING GAS BOTTLE	30.00		1192.94	*Heating gas – Use home allowance*
22-04-20XX	DD	TESCO MOBILE 1234567895	8.70		1222.94	*Groceries*
22-04-20XX	DEB	ASDA PETROL 4415 CD 7025	24.76		1231.64	*Petrol BUT – Use car allowance*
21-04-20XX	BGC	SAINSBURY AB950		489.15	1256.40	*Sainsburys Pay*
18-04-20XX	DEB	E H BOOTH & CO CD 7025	8.99		767.25	*Groceries*
15-04-20XX	DD	HALIFAX INSURANCE C1234	30.00		776.24	*Home Insurance – Use home all'ce*
13-04-20XX	DD	SKY DIGITAL 002212345678	58.25		806.24	*SKY Subscription*
12-04-20XX	DEB	SAINSBURY'S S/MKT CD 522	24.45		864.49	*Groceries*
12-04-20XX	DEB	LIDL UK CD 7025	3.27		888.94	*Groceries*
11-04-20XX	DEB	OCADO RETAIL LIMIT CD 52.	36.09		892.21	*Wine*
11-04-20XX	DEB	DVLA VEHICLE TAX CD 7025	145.00		928.30	*Use car allowance instead*
07-04-20XX	CPT	LNK SPAR - THREE W CD 522	50.00		1073.30	*Cash for personal use*
05-04-20XX	DEB	STATIONERY SUPPLIES	16.54		1123.30	*Printer Paper?*
04-04-20XX	PAY	BANK FEE	5.00		1139.84	*Bank Fee*
01-04-20XX	DD	BT GROUP PLC MR73278384	51.16		1144.84	*Split*
01-04-20XX	SO	OXFAM	4.00		1196.00	*Charity donation*

You can first examine the bank statement and try and work out which might be business expenses and which might be personal and which might be business income? What do you think about the Car Tax and Home Insurance? There seems to be a Simplex style form category for Motor Expenses so why has Louise marked these as 'Use Car Allowance instead'? And what about Premises Costs on the Simplex style form?

Louise has made some notes at the side of her bank statement lines so that she can see which are personal items.

Going up the statement looking for personal items she can see that all the Groceries are personal and on 07-04-20XX some cash for personal use was taken out of a cash machine.

She bought some wine on 11-04-20XX and the SKY bill is for the television channels. Louise got her Sainsbury's pay on 21-04-20XX. She makes a monthly charity contribution to Oxfam. She is not sure about some items such as the possible printer paper on 05-04-20XX. She will need to check her business paperwork.

Simplified Expenses

Louise has opted to use the HMRC new 'Simplified Expenses Accounting' for her self-employed business tax return so whilst she has some bank statement items for petrol she will not count them as the 'Simplified Expenses' uses the car use allowance based on business mileage.

She will also not count heating oil or house insurance since again she will use the 'Simplified Expenses' home use allowance based on the hours she spends working at home on business matters.

'Simplified expenses' mean just that. You do not have the extra work and paperwork sorting out which part of the home has to share the cost of rent, rates, insurance, heating, lighting, etc. and also do not have to track car repairs, insurance, petrol, etc.

This saves time but you can opt to do the not simplified version if you wish. We are going to use the 'simplified expenses' in this book, since most sole traders do not run a pottery with a furnace eating up electricity with high insurance costs!

We are now going to concentrate on just the items that relate to the business, although Louise will keep a copy of the full bank statement in her bookkeeping record keeping system.

The business items and amounts paid in or out are the ones left on the bank statement below. They are just for the business and those payments out that are SHARED with the business. The business items and part shares will need entering into the Simplex Cash Book into the latest week's page.

Date	Type	Description	Out (£)	In (£)	
30-04-2	DD	CREDIT CARD COMPANY	72.6		Postage paid by credit card
28-04-2	CR	PAYPAL TRANSFER		560	Transfer IN of some of the PayPal balance
25-04-2	DEB	SPANISH SHOES	417.6		Purchases of stock
05-04-2	DEB	STATIONERY SUPPLIES	16.54		Printer Paper? *Check this!*
04-04-2	PAY	BANK FEE	5		Bank Fee
01-04-2	DD	BT GROUP PLC MR73278384-C	51.16		Split? *And this!*

When you create a new record of a transaction in your books you are entering amounts and dates and purpose of business money in to the Cash Book using the 'cash basis' accounting system which needs the details of the exact date when the bill was paid or the money received. These payment dates are on the bank statement and other statements.

Louise needs to therefore now go through her business files folder to find the relevant invoices and source documents to support her view that all these remaining bank statement entries are wholly business related and then find the date they were paid. We will look at how this is done shortly.

This checking is useful since by checking her files of business source documents and reconciling with the bank statement, she may find that she has some unpaid invoices that are not accounted for on the bank statement. They will need dealing with at some stage too.

Summary

In this section the Case Study was introduced and we looked at the flow of paperwork and reconciliation between bank transactions and the supporting paperwork for money out. The Simplex style of Cash Book forms was explained.

It is important to remember that bookkeeping is the making of a new record about a financial transaction. It is not a new transaction. It is a record about a transaction.

You make the record in one of a list of HMRC approved categories in a Cash Book once you can show that the transaction took place using supporting source documents which you then file correctly.

So the steps in the bookkeeping process broadly involve:

Obtaining the source documents that are records of a financial transaction and then examining the records for evidence of the transaction taking place.

This is then followed by 'Posting' a new record of the transaction before filing the source documents correctly for future reference

We will spend much of the rest of this training book using these steps.

We will now practice bookkeeping using the Simplex style of cash book and the Case Study source records. You can print the training files business documents and Cash Book forms (by request by emailing the author) so that you can try posting some Cash Book entries yourself. Or just keep reading about the methods and practise later.

Chapter Six – Case Study Sales and Purchases Bookkeeping

> **What you will find in this section**
> - ✓ **Sales Bookkeeping**
> - ✓ **Purchases Bookkeeping**
> - ✓ **eBay Fees**
> - ✓ **PayPal Fees**

Although you have already tried your hand at a bit of bookkeeping entries (bookkeeping postings), we are going to now attend to the Case Study in a set way of working our way though Sales, Expense Purchases and Stock Purchases. So you will be repeating some postings.

Sales Invoices – Money In Bookkeeping

Bearing in mind that the bookkeeping process starts with obtaining the source documents that are records of a financial transaction, we naturally think that a 'money in' transaction must start with the sending of a source document to the customer in the form of a Sales Invoice like the one below from the Case Study:

Invoice

Businessshoes
Be Smart and Comfortable

Date: 24th April 20X
Invoice #: 0125
Customer ID: C0125

To:
Adam Smith
15 Oxford Rd
Hampton Poyle
Kidlington
Oxfordshire
OX5 2QD

Ship to:
Adam Smith
15 Oxford Rd
Hampton Poyle
Kidlington
Oxfordshire
OX5 2QD

Paid

Salesperson	Job	Shipping Method	Shipping Term	Delivery Date	Payment Terms	Due Date
		Next Day signed	Free Postage	25th April 20XX	Paypal	Paid

Qty	Item #	Description	Unit Price	Discount	Line Total
1.00	OX0C	Oxford Size 9 Black	£ 74.60		£ 74.60

Total Discount

Subtotal £ 74.60
Sales Tax
Total £ 74.60
Total Owed 0.00

Make all payments via Paypal to this email address: lbrown1947@outlook.com
Thank you for your business!

3 St Georges Grove, Greasby, Wirral, Merseyside CH46 6DD, UK

Indeed many bookkeeping systems encourage the idea of registering the fact that the customer has been sent the goods and a Sales Invoice which we expect to be paid in full. You will see later that the spreadsheet version of a Cash Book system, provided free with this kit, has a worksheet that tracks Sales Invoices and when they are due to be paid along with the actual payment.

Whilst it is a always good thing to know if you have been paid for the goods or services that you have provided, an eBay trader using PayPal will generally have payment before the goods are sent. If you do not get paid by PayPal or cash, and get bank transfers or cheques you may wish to check that you have got the money in your bank account before you send any goods to new customers.

PayPal statement

We naturally want to know if we have been paid for our goods or services via PayPal and the best way, for an eBay trader like Louise to find out as part of a bookkeeping routine, is to go to our PayPal account and then download a copy of our account statement which is shown below for the Case Study for the last week in April, which is the same period that Louise has a set of Sales Invoices for.

To find out how our Case Study trader downloaded the PayPal statements go to Chapter 14.

Date	Time	Time Z	Name	Type	Status	Curre	Gross	Fee	From To Em	Trans
30-04-2	12:45:00	BST	STEPHEN	PayPa	Comp	GBP	60	-2.24	STEVEE29@	4VV66
29-04-2	11:45:00	BST	ALAN AVE	PayPa	Comp	GBP	74.6	-2.34	ALanAlbrowi	8HRD9
28-04-2	21:55:00	BST	PETER AL!	PayPa	Comp	GBP	74.6	-2.34	PandElbrowi	6BJI12
28-04-2	11:55:00	BST	MATT LEE	PayPa	Comp	GBP	74.6	-2.34	MLEE:lbrowi	5GGI4
28-04-2	20:14:52	BST	Bank Accc	Withd	Comp	GBP	-560	0		4U810
28-04-2	17:55:00	BST	DAN KNO	PayPa	Comp	GBP	74.6	-2.34	DKNO lbrowi	6SJU3
28-04-2	9:55:00	BST	CARL PEA	PayPa	Comp	GBP	74.6	-2.34	CP123 lbrowi	6ugc2
27-04-2	11:55:00	BST	CONNOR	PayPa	Comp	GBP	74.6	-2.34	CCCCrlbrowi	4AGU:
25-04-2	9:17:15	BST	KEITH BAI	PayPa	Comp	GBP	74.6	-2.34	kb123 lbrowi	3R050
25-04-2	10:50:45	BST	CARL LYM	PayPa	Comp	GBP	74.6	-2.34	Calrar lbrowi	2CY34
25-04-2	22:52:23	BST	NICHOLA!	PayPa	Comp	GBP	74.6	-2.34	NBB@ lbrowi	4CX34
25-04-2	23:55:00	BST	FRANK W	PayPa	Comp	GBP	74.6	-2.34	Franklbrowi	3CFY3
24-04-2	9:31:40	BST	ADAM SM	PayPa	Comp	GBP	74.6	-2.34	adam:lbrowi	7MF9:
23-04-2	10:31:40	BST	FRANCES	PayPa	Comp	GBP	74.6	-2.34	fpoolelbrowi	7MF9:
22-04-2	11:31:40	BST	SID JAME:	PayPa	Comp	GBP	74.6	-2.34	sbJamlbrowi	7MF9:
21-04-2	12:31:40	BST	PAUL MIL	PayPa	Comp	GBP	74.6	-2.34	Pjmillelbrowi	7MF9:
20-04-2	13:31:40	BST	SCOTT JO	PayPa	Comp	GBP	74.6	-2.34	scottielbrowi	7MF9:
19-04-2	14:31:40	BST	LINUS PAl	PayPa	Comp	GBP	74.6	-2.34	lpauli:lbrowi	7MF9:
19-04-2	15:31:40	BST	GERRY RC	PayPa	Comp	GBP	74.6	-2.34	grolanlbrowi	7MF9:
17-04-2	11:55:00	BST	eBay	PayPa	Comp	GBP	-102.05	0		34F32

It is a relatively easy matter to reconcile this week's 12 Sales Invoices No's 0125 to 0136 with the transactions of money into our PayPal account according to the statement. All the invoices are in the set of files by request from the author. We can see that the names of the customers and the amounts match up using the GROSS column on the PayPal statement which is the same figure on the sales invoices in our weekly folder.

We are going to now post the week of sales income into our Simplex style Cash Book using the Receipts form shown below which you can get from the author by email request.

Week No   Commencing

Day	Date	Daily Takings		Other Receipts	Particulars of Other Receipts	Lottery etc Takings
		Cash Col 1	Cheques, Credit & Debit Cards Col 2	Col 3		Col 4
Sub Total					Totals	
Grss Wkly Tak's(1+2)						

Posting the transactions requires a total for each day of the week in a Simplex form, so bits of adding up to do here.

If you are using the training materials you can either add up the Sales Invoices for each date, or use the PayPal statement above to come to the total for the week of £880.60 as shown in the completed form below.

There is nothing to stop you just putting the total at the end of the week.

One of the benefits of a spreadsheet or QuickBooks is that the adding up is done for you – although you can still make mistakes entering data in any system.

Week 11 Commencing 24th April 20XX

Day	Date	Receipts				
		Daily Takings		Other Receipts	Particulars of Other Receipts	Lottery etc Takings
		Cash Col 1	Cheques, Credit & Debit Cards Col 2	Col 3		Col 4
Mon	24th April	74·60				
Tue	25th April	298·40				
Wed	26th April	74·60				
Thu	27th April	0·00				
Fri	28th April	298·40				
Sat	29th April	74·60				
Sun	30th April	60·00				
	Sub Total	880·60	0·00	0·00	Totals	0.00
	Gross Weekly Takings (col 1+2)		880·60			

Whilst all the sales invoices we had have matched the PayPal Gross receipts this week; this will not always be the case. You may not have been paid for all your sales invoices and this system of keeping the issued sales invoices in a folder and then checking for the actual money in is a good one to use that reminds us if necessary to chase up late or partial payments. There is another important item to note and that is that we use the Gross column on the PayPal statement and not the Net column after PayPal fees.

Gross is what must be entered as sales income into the Cash Book and <u>never</u> Net.

If you do not sell on eBay then you will need to check that you have been paid before you enter any sale in your books. If you have been paid by cash then you will need to issue a receipt to the customer and keep a copy yourself, with a note on it that it has been paid. If you are paid by bank transfer then you will check your bank statement. If you are paid by cheque then you will again need to check you bank statement after you have paid the check into the bank.

Car boot Sale Stock Purchases

We have had a simple situation for Louise as far as purchase invoice paperwork is concerned for items that are business stock. But what if her business was based on buying from car boot sales, paying in cash and then selling the purchases? Where is the paperwork then? There is no invoice from the supplier and no money out on the bank statement.

The best way to run an eBay trader business that uses cash is to use a kitty or float type system - an imprest petty cash system (imprest just means a loan)and a pad of petty cash voucher slips which cost a couple of pounds from a stationers.

You begin by withdrawing say £200 from your bank account - from an ATM. Keep the bank withdrawal printout slip.
Then put the £200 in a tin (your petty cash tin) along with the bank withdrawal slip. Now when you buy an item from a car boot sale with some of your own cash (not the cash in the tin), you must make a note of the item on a petty cash voucher from your petty cash voucher pad, with the date, the item details, the car boot sale name and the cost. When you get home put the petty cash voucher into the tin and take out the same exact cash amount spent to replace your personal funds.

At the end of a week you can total all your purchases on a blank A4 sheet of paper that acts as your purchase invoices record, with the petty cash vouchers stapled to it. Your total purchases amount and your balance of cash left in the petty cash tin should add up to £200 at all times. You will need to top up your petty cash tin back to £200 by an ATM cash withdrawal every few week or so.

If your tin is missing some cash from the total or you have lost a petty cash slip or some cash one week then you will not be able to claim the cost of the purchase and will have to bear the cost yourself. So keep track of all cash purchases.

Purchases Bookkeeping for the Case Study

Having completed the sales bookkeeping we turn our attention to the Case Study purchases – the expenses.

We return to the bank statement source document below where, for ease of use, we now just show the business related lines. We will now work our way forward, in order of date paid, according to the bank statement and search through the collection of UNPAID EXPENSES INVOICES in our weekly document files or at the front of our Lever Arch Files where we keep our files. Filing is discussed in more detail in its own chapter later.

Telephone

Since we are interested in the date order of purchase invoices we should start with the earliest date on the bank statement – the phone bill for £51.16 on the 1st April 20XX.

Louise has made a comment SPLIT. This is because she knows that the telephone line and calls and broadband are not WHOLLY AND EXCLUSIVELY for business use. HMRC rules mean that she cannot claim the whole amount if some of the cost is for personal use, so she must SPLIT the cost and share it between her personal and business costs.
Louise has an Internet based telephone account and she has downloaded and printed out a copy of the bill which is shown below in parts. You can see the whole bill in the Appendix.

Date	Type	Description	Out (£)	In (£)	
30-04-2	DD	CREDIT CARD COMPANY	72.6		*Postage paid by credit card*
28-04-2	CR	PAYPAL TRANSFER		560	*Transfer IN of some of the PayPal balance*
25-04-2	DEB	SPANISH SHOES	417.6		*Purchases of stock*
05-04-2	DEB	STATIONERY SUPPLIES	16.54		*Printer Paper?* (And this!)
04-04-2	PAY	BANK FEE	5		*Bank Fee*
01-04-2	DD	BT GROUP PLC MR73278384-C	51.16		*Split?* (Check this!)

Bill reference: Bill date: 05 May 20XX

Telephone and Broadband Rental and other charges
Phone line – 0151623405
Line Rental
05 May - 04 Jun 201XX

£0.00

Because you've got Line Rental Saver your line rental is paid until
26 Mar 20XX
Package
Broadband and Calls
05 May –04 Jun 20XX. This is the cost of your Package at £21.80 a month charged in advance
- **Calling Plan** Unlimited Evening and Weekend Plan
- **Broadband** Unlimited Broadband

£21.80

Part One

There are a few items of note here.

First the line rental cost is zero as the line rental has been paid earlier in March to get a discount so we need to make sure that the cost back then has been accounted for in the Cash Book and that we have the paperwork – bill and bank statement. The line rental cost will need to be SPLIT between the business and personal expense. The cost also spans two tax years (which last from April to April) so it may be necessary to work out how much of the cost belongs to this year and how much to last year.

Secondly the shared business and personal Broadband and Calls are a PHONE PACKAGE, and so this makes it hard to then say how much belongs to the business. HMRC expect you to be reasonable. It would NOT BE REASONABLE to charge 90% to the business and 10% to personal if she has no evidence to back up her claim.

The bill element of £21.80 for broadband also needs some evidence for the personal and business shares.

Louise has made some diary entries where she has noted the number of hours she spent each day this week on business use of her Internet connected computer managing her sole trader business adverts and sales. She also makes a note of how much daily computer time she spent this week playing Candy Crush. She summarises the hours that week on an A4 sheet and files it with the telephone bill. Louise estimates that 40% of the broadband time was for business use and so the cost for the business should be £21.80 x 0.4 = £8.72.

Part Two

Sport
Sport Pack
05 May – 04 Jun 20XX. This is the cost of your Sport on the Digital Satellite Platform at £5.00 a month, charged in advance from 05 May 20XX to 04 Jun 20XX

£5.00

Sport HD Pack05
05 May – 04 Jun 20XX. This is the cost of your Sport HD Pack at £4.00 a month, charged in advance from 05 May 20XX to 04 Jun 20XX
£4.00
Mobile
Mobile 500MB Plan 01234 5678910
05 May - 04 Jun 20XX . This is the cost of your mobile plan at £10.00

£10.00

Neither the two TV Sports costs nor the Mobile (phone) Louise uses personally are classed as business use, so all this £5 + £4 + £10 = £19 total is a personal cost.

Part Three

```
Broadband Discount 0151623405
05 May - 04 Jun 16
Because you have our broadband your mobile bill is less
                                                    -£5.00
Total rental and other charges
                                                    £35.80
Phone usage for 0151623405
You made 18 call(s) - number of free call(s)4.
                                                    £15.23
Mobile usage for 01234 5678910
                                                    £0.14
Charges not covered by your mobile plan.
0 minutes, 8 messages, 0MB data

Total usage charges
                                                    £15.36
Total including any applicable taxes                £51.16
```

The discount is for the mobile phone and is because the customer has the same company for broadband. This reduces the personal mobile phone bill so does not affect business expenses. The 14p for mobile texts not covered in the mobile phone monthly plan is also a personal cost.

There were 18 calls on the land line costing £15.23. Louise keeps track in her diary of any business calls to the wholesaler. There were 4 business calls (or 22%) this month and so she reckons that the business is responsible for £15.23 x 0.22 = £3.35.

The total split of the £51.16 that belongs to the business is then £8.72 + £3.35 = £12.07 for April 20XX. Louise can enter this into her Simplex Cash Book for this week, although the cost covers the whole month.

A final point about phone and broadband bills is that the line rental and subscriptions to broadband are paid in advance.

So we pay for May in April. For the self-employed trader who uses the cash accounting system this timing of expenses does not matter. However if you are running a Limited Company with accrual accounting then the advance payments would be seen as prepayments whose cost would belong to following month

Although the bank statement does not show a payment for £12.07 Louise sees that the total bill of £51.16 was paid on the 1st April 20XX and so now Louise can tick the line on the bank statement, make notes about her calculations of the £12.07 on the back of the telephone bill invoice and then stamp the telephone bill as PAID with the date of 1st April 20XX and then file it at the back of her Purchase Invoices 20XX Lever Arch File on top of the March Paid Purchase Invoices.

Bank Fee

This is an easy one to enter since it appears on the bank statement as £5 on 04/04/20XX. But does all of this belong to the business? There is no line for bank fees on the Simplex 'Payments other than for Stock' Form so Louise enters a new category of Bank Fees below the Other Expenses category. There is no purchase invoice for this or a till receipt.
 Louise did not initially mark the bank fee as SPLIT but having just done the phone bill she feels that perhaps 80% of the bank entries are related to her personal spending and 20% to the business and so she charges her Cash Book new Bank Fees line with only £1 for the last week of April 20XX. With no purchase invoice to file Louise needs a record so she makes a second copy of the bank statement, makes a note of the 20% business share on it and uses that as an invoice for the bank charges of £1.

She stamps it as Paid and then adds the date of the payment and files this second copy in the PAID section behind the cardboard divider in her Purchase Invoices 20XX Lever Arch File and continues to work with the first copy of the bank statement until it can be filed in her Box File 20XX where she keeps all bank statements for the year.
Louise in effect has used a copy of the bank statement with the bank fee on it as a purchase invoice for her records.

Stationery

Louise was not sure if the next bank statement money out to Stationery Supplies of £16.54 was wholly for business or was personal use. It depended on what the bank statement amount was for and she needed to check the invoices in her weekly folder. It was paid on 15/04/20XX according to the bank statement and looking through her paperwork folder she finds the following purchase invoice.

Stationery Supplies Co
Invoice for
Your order of 05 April, 2| Order ID 202-0661704-3052340   Invoice number DYTMSDRGb
Invoice date 05 April, 20XX
Qty. Item   Our Pric VAT Rat Total Price
      (excl. VAT)
          1 5 Star Office Value Copier Paper   20% £16.54
Wrapped 75gsm A4 White - 1 box containing 5 Reams of 500 sheets
Office Product. B000I6QZNM : 5018206085030
Shipping charges   £0.00   £0.00

Subtotal (excl. VAT)	Subtotal (excl. VAT)	VAT at	Total VAT	Total
0%	20%	20%	£2.76	£16.54
£0.00	£13.78	£2.76		

Conversion rate - £1.00 : EUR 1,29
This shipment completes your order which has been paid
Balance to Pay   £0.00

This invoice was for printer paper for the business which Louise uses so she can print out Sales Invoices for customers. There are then no complications or splitting with this invoice so Louise can enter the amount of £16.54 into her Cash Book in the 'Payments other than for Stock' Form on the Stationery, etc. sub category and stamp the invoice as PAID with the date as 05th April 20XX. She can then file it in her Purchase Invoices 20XX Lever Arch file at the back.

Her Cash Book 'Payments other than for Stock' Form now looks like this:

Simplex Book Page Weekly Layout Style

Payments other than for Stock			
Nature of Payment	Cash Col 11		Cheques, credit and debit cards Col 12
Employment Cost (i) Wages			
(ii) Inland Revenue PAYE &NI			
Premises Cost (i) Rent and Rates			
(ii) Light, Heat and Insurance			
(iii) Cleaning			
Repairs			
Gen.Admin. (i) Telephone *and Broadband*	12	07	
(ii) Postage			
(iii) Stationery, etc.	16	54	
Motor Expenses (i) Fuel			
(ii) Servicing & Repairs, etc			
Travel & Subsistence			
Advertising & Entertainment			
Legal and Professional			
Interest Payable			
Bank Fees	1	00	

Purchase of Stock

Louise has a Purchase Invoice in her business documents folder for an amount of £417.60 from her wholesaler Spanish Shoes for the last week in April.

Spanish Shoes — Invoice

Invoice To:
Mrs. L. Brown
Businessshoes
3 St Georges Grove
Greasby
Wirral
Merseyside
CH46 6DD
UK
Phone
Customer ID

Delivery Address:
Mrs. L. Brown
Businessshoes
3 St Georges Grove
Greasby
Wirral
Merseyside
CH46 6DD
UK
Phone
Customer ID

Date: 25/04/20XX
Customer #: 7804
Invoice #: 0420
Terms: Cash Account

Qty	Item No	Description	Unit Price £	Total £
4	P14001/09	Mens Derby Lace Up Black Size 9	29.00	116.00
4	P12001/10	Mens Oxford Lace Up Black Size 10	29.00	116.00
4	P14001/11	Mens Derby Lace Up Black Size 11	29.00	116.00
			Subtotal	348.00
			VAT	69.60
			Total	£ 417.60

Make all cheques payable to Spanishshoes
Thank you for your business!

Spanish Shoes Ltd, Seven Acres Business Park, Woodbridge IP12 4PS, UK

This matches the amount and payee on her bank statement below dated 25/04/201XX so she can enter the £417.60 into her Cash Book using the 'Payments for Business Stock' Form and then stamp the invoice as PAID with the date of 25/04/20XX.

Date	Type	Description	Out (£)	In (£)	
30-04-2	DD	CREDIT CARD COMPANY	72.6		*Postage paid by credit card*
28-04-2	CR	PAYPAL TRANSFER		560	*Transfer IN of some of the PayPal balance*
25-04-2	DEB	SPANISH SHOES	417.6		*Purchases of stock*
05-04-2	DEB	STATIONERY SUPPLIES	16.54		*Printer Paper?* (And this!)
04-04-2	PAY	BANK FEE	5		*Bank Fee*
01-04-2	DD	BT GROUP PLC MR73278384-C	51.16		*Split?* (Check this!)

She can then file the invoice at the back of her Purchase Invoices 20XX Lever Arch File. Louise has to write in the date paid of 25/04/20XX into the form and also the name of the firm that was paid of 'Spanish Shoes'. Note that we did not put any payee details or specific payment dates of the week in the 'Payments other than for Stock' Form earlier, but in every case we have kept the invoice filed in the Lever Arch Files in case of a query from HMRC.

Her Simplex Cash Book 'Payments for Business Stock' Form now looks like this.

Payments for Business Stock			
Date or Chq No	To whom paid	Cash Col 9	Cheques, credit and debit cards Col 10
25/04/20XX	Spanish Shoes	417 60	

Simplex Style Payments for Business Stock

The sales and purchases we have posted in the books so far have been all supported by Invoices of one sort of another where we send the customer an invoice or the supplier sends us an invoice and these both take place around the date of the sale and we get a document. However we saw that with the bank fee there was no invoice, but just a deduction from our bank balance.

Now if we sell on eBay we also incur costs both from eBay and PayPal and neither of them send us an immediate invoice.

We need some source documents about eBay and PayPal charges. If you do not sell on eBay or get paid by PayPal you can skip the next section which deals with the situation where the expense money is automatically taken from our PayPal account balance. It also deals with how we obtain some of these supporting documents that we need.

Chapter Seven – Less Tax – eBay and PayPal Fees

Advertising Expenses

We can see in the Simplex style Cash Book that the 'Payments other than for Stock' has a section for Advertising and Entertainment.

Simplex Book Page Weekly Layout Style
Last Week in May 20XX

Nature of Payment	Cash Col 11	Cheques, credit and debit cards Col 12
Employment Cost (i) Wages		
(ii) Inland Revenue PAYE &NI		
Premises Cost (i) Rent and Rates		
(ii) Light, Heat and Insurance		
(iii) Cleaning		
Repairs		
Gen.Admin. (i) Telephone		
(ii) Postage		
(iii) Stationery, etc.		
Motor Expenses (i) Fuel		
(ii) Servicing & Repairs, etc		
Travel & Subsistence		
Advertising & Entertainment		
Legal and Professional		
Interest Payable *PayPal and bank fees*		
Other Expenses		
Lottery Prizes Paid		
Scratch Cards Prizes Paid		
Ebay Final Value Fees		
Car Mileage Allowance		
Working from home allowance		
Totals		

However HMRC has banned entertainment (Boo!) as an allowable expense so we can only enter advertising costs in the Simplex style form.

PayPal advertising is when we list an item to sell and have to pay listing fees to eBay, whether we sell the item or not.

Louise pays for an eBay 'Basic Business' listing subscription which gives her 200 listings each month for £19.99 (2016). She has an invoice from eBay in her weekly document folder, shown below which includes costs for both the subscription and the so called 'Final Value Fees' which we refer to in this book as 'merchant services' expenses which require special treatment in order to avoid paying more income tax on business profits than is necessary. We explain merchant services later on.

Invoice number
083115-79019712345

INVOICE
31 March 20XX

Account summary   01 March – 31 March Pacific Time
New fees Includes promotional savings and United Kingdom VAT at the applicable rate.
BasicBusiness Shop Advance Monthly Subscription for April 20XX £19.99
Final value fees £82.06
Subtotal £102.05
Total due £102.05
Do you have a question about the total amount due? We're help!
You have set up an automatic payment method. Your invoice amount will be automatically
 deducted from your account between 15 April 20XX and 17 April 20XX.
 account between 15 April 20XX and 17 April 20XX.
 The amount deducted may vary based on recent payments or credits.
 Make a onetime payment
 Change your payment details
Promotional savings (View details)
Insertion fees -£0.00
Advanced listing upgrade fees -£0.00
Total Saved** -£0.00

**Total saved is an estimate and may not include all promotions credits or reflect changes
 in your eligibility for promotions

Here we can see that the invoice is for a total of £102.05, that includes £19.99 for the Basic Business Shop Advance subscription for April 20XX for the Case Study business.

Whilst we have the invoice source record, we do not know if it has been paid and for this we need to refer to the Case Study PayPal statement or the bank statement. This is because PayPal automatically take the total eBay invoice expenses from your PayPal account balance about two weeks after the end of a trading month.

Here is a copy of the PayPal account for April below:

Date	Time	Time Z	Name	Type	Status	Curre	Gross	Fee	From	To En	Trans
30-04-2	12:45:00	BST	STEPHEN	PayPa	Comp	GBP	60	-2.24	STEVEE29@		4VV6E
29-04-2	11:45:00	BST	ALAN AVE	PayPa	Comp	GBP	74.6	-2.34	ALanA	lbrow	8HRD9
28-04-2	21:55:00	BST	PETER AL!	PayPa	Comp	GBP	74.6	-2.34	PandE	lbrow	6BJI12
28-04-2	11:55:00	BST	MATT LEE	PayPa	Comp	GBP	74.6	-2.34	MLEE:	lbrow	5GGI4
28-04-2	20:14:52	BST	Bank Acc(	Withd	Comp	GBP	-560	0			4U810
28-04-2	17:55:00	BST	DAN KNO	PayPa	Comp	GBP	74.6	-2.34	DKNO	lbrow	6SJU3
28-04-2	9:55:00	BST	CARL PEA	PayPa	Comp	GBP	74.6	-2.34	CP123	lbrow	6ugc2
27-04-2	11:55:00	BST	CONNOR	PayPa	Comp	GBP	74.6	-2.34	CCCCr	lbrow	4AGU:
25-04-2	9:17:15	BST	KEITH BAI	PayPa	Comp	GBP	74.6	-2.34	kb123	lbrow	3R050
25-04-2	10:50:45	BST	CARL LYM	PayPa	Comp	GBP	74.6	-2.34	Calrar	lbrow	2CY34
25-04-2	22:52:23	BST	NICHOLA!	PayPa	Comp	GBP	74.6	-2.34	NBB@	lbrow	4CX34
25-04-2	23:55:00	BST	FRANK W	PayPa	Comp	GBP	74.6	-2.34	Frankl	lbrow	3CFY3
24-04-2	9:31:40	BST	ADAM SN	PayPa	Comp	GBP	74.6	-2.34	adam:	lbrow	7MF9:
23-04-2	10:31:40	BST	FRANCES	PayPa	Comp	GBP	74.6	-2.34	fpoole	lbrow	7MF9:
22-04-2	11:31:40	BST	SID JAME:	PayPa	Comp	GBP	74.6	-2.34	sbJam	lbrow	7MF9:
21-04-2	12:31:40	BST	PAUL MIL	PayPa	Comp	GBP	74.6	-2.34	Pjmille	lbrow	7MF9:
20-04-2	13:31:40	BST	SCOTT JO	PayPa	Comp	GBP	74.6	-2.34	scottie	lbrow	7MF9:
19-04-2	14:31:40	BST	LINUS PAI	PayPa	Comp	GBP	74.6	-2.34	lpauli:	lbrow	7MF9:
19-04-2	15:31:40	BST	GERRY RC	PayPa	Comp	GBP	74.6	-2.34	grolan	lbrow	7MF9:
17-04-2	11:55:00	BST	eBay	PayPa	Comp	GBP	-102.05	0			34F32

You can see that the amount of £102.05 was deducted from the account balance on 17/04/20XX.

We can now post the advertising fee of £19.99 in our Cash Book since we know it was paid (deducted) as part of the eBay invoice payment for £102.05.

Simplex Book Page Weekly Layout Style

Payments other than for Stock				
Nature of Payment		Cash Col 11		Cheques, credit and debit cards Col 12
Employment Cost (i) Wages				
(ii) Inland Revenue PAYE &NI				
Premises Cost (i) Rent and Rates				
(ii) Light, Heat and Insurance				
(iii) Cleaning				
Repairs				
Gen.Admin. (i) Telephone and Broadband		12	07	
(ii) Postage				
(iii) Stationery, etc.		16	54	
Motor Expenses (i) Fuel				
(ii) Servicing & Repairs, etc				
Travel & Subsistence				
Advertising & Entertainment - eBay Basic Business Subs		19	99	
Legal and Professional				
Interest Payable				
Bank Fees		1	00	

106

PayPal Fees are Cost of Sales - A Special Type of Expense

In the PayPal statement shown below we see the payment of the eBay invoice on 17/04/20XX of £102.05 of which £19.99 was for eBay advertising fees.

Date	Time	Time Z	Name	Type	Status	Curre	Gross	Fee	From	To	Em Trans
30-04-2	12:45:00	BST	STEPHEN	PayPa	Comp	GBP	60	-2.24	STEVEE29@	4VV66	
29-04-2	11:45:00	BST	ALAN AVE	PayPa	Comp	GBP	74.6	-2.34	ALanA	brow	8HRD9
28-04-2	21:55:00	BST	PETER AL!	PayPa	Comp	GBP	74.6	-2.34	PandE	brow	6BJI12
28-04-2	11:55:00	BST	MATT LEE	PayPa	Comp	GBP	74.6	-2.34	MLEE:	brow	5GGI4
28-04-2	20:14:52	BST	Bank Acc	Withd	Comp	GBP	-560	0			4U810
28-04-2	17:55:00	BST	DAN KNO	PayPa	Comp	GBP	74.6	-2.34	DKNO	brow	6SJU3
28-04-2	9:55:00	BST	CARL PEA	PayPa	Comp	GBP	74.6	-2.34	CP123	brow	6ugc2
27-04-2	11:55:00	BST	CONNOR	PayPa	Comp	GBP	74.6	-2.34	CCCCr	brow	4AGU:
25-04-2	9:17:15	BST	KEITH BAI	PayPa	Comp	GBP	74.6	-2.34	kb123	brow	3R050
25-04-2	10:50:45	BST	CARL LYM	PayPa	Comp	GBP	74.6	-2.34	Calrar	brow	2CY34
25-04-2	22:52:23	BST	NICHOLA!	PayPa	Comp	GBP	74.6	-2.34	NBB@	brow	4CX34
25-04-2	23:55:00	BST	FRANK W	PayPa	Comp	GBP	74.6	-2.34	Frankl	brow	3CFY3
24-04-2	9:31:40	BST	ADAM SN	PayPa	Comp	GBP	74.6	-2.34	adam:	brow	7MF9:
23-04-2	10:31:40	BST	FRANCES	PayPa	Comp	GBP	74.6	-2.34	fpoole	brow	7MF9:
22-04-2	11:31:40	BST	SID JAME	PayPa	Comp	GBP	74.6	-2.34	sbJam	brow	7MF9:
21-04-2	12:31:40	BST	PAUL MIL	PayPa	Comp	GBP	74.6	-2.34	Pjmille	brow	7MF9:
20-04-2	13:31:40	BST	SCOTT JO	PayPa	Comp	GBP	74.6	-2.34	scottie	brow	7MF9:
19-04-2	14:31:40	BST	LINUS PAL	PayPa	Comp	GBP	74.6	-2.34	lpauli:	brow	7MF9:
19-04-2	15:31:40	BST	GERRY RC	PayPa	Comp	GBP	74.6	-2.34	grolan	brow	7MF9:
17-04-2	11:55:00	BST	eBay	PayPa	Comp	GBP	-102.05	0			34F32

But did you notice that on every line of the PayPal statement, where we had some sales income from customers, there was Fee deduction by PayPal of £2.34 on every sale for £74.60. This deduction was a charge of about 3% by PayPal for their merchant handling services.

Many eBay traders are confused about how to treat these PayPal fees in their books since PayPal seems to behave a bit like a bank and the nearest HMRC expenses item in their list on the annual self employed business tax return form SA103S extract below looks like the item in box 17, that of Interest and bank and credit card, etc. financial charges. PayPal fees do seem like financial charges.

Business income – if your annual business turnover was below £85,000

9 Your turnover - the takings, fees, sales or money earned by your business
£ 3 3 5 7 0 · 0 0

10.1 Trading income allowance - read notes
£ 0 · 0 0

10 Any Other Business income not included in box 9
£ 0 · 0 0

Allowable business expenses
If your annual turnover was below £85,000 you may just put your total expenses in box 20, rather than filling in the whole section.

11 Cost of goods bought for resale or goods used
£ · 0 0

16 Accountancy, legal and other professional fees
£ · 0 0

12 Car, van and travel expenses after private use proportion
£ · 0 0

17 Interest and bank and credit card financial charges
£ · 0 0

13 Wages, salaries and other staff costs
£ · 0 0

18 Phone, fax, stationery and other office costs
£ · 0 0

14 Rent, rates, power and insurance costs
£ · 0 0

19 Other allowable business expenses - client entertaining costs are not an allowable expense
£ · 0 0

15 Repairs and renewals of property and equipment
£ · 0 0

20 Total allowable expenses - total of boxes 11 to 19
£ 2 4 5 0 0 · 0 0

SA103S 2019
HMRC 12/18

Net Profit or Loss

21 Net Profit - if your business income is more than your expenses (if box 9+box 10 minus box 20 is positive)
£ 9 0 6 5 · 0 0

22 Or, net loss - if your expenses exceed your business income (if box 20 minus (box 9 plus box 10) is positive)
£ · 0 0

However whilst it may seem a good idea to consider PayPal merchanting services fees as financial charges, there is a limit to what these can be of £500 a year (2016).

That means that if you posted PayPal fees on every transaction, once you sold more than £16,667 of sales in a year, then your £500 limit would be breached and you would pay tax on any more fees.

It actually gets much much worse than that since there is another fee from eBay for each sale of 10% of the gross income.

If you also treated eBay final value fees as financial charges you would exceed your £500 tax free limit on the total PayPal and eBay fees once you sold more than £3847 worth of goods and pay tax on any further eBay and PayPal fees.

Clearly then we need to find another allowable expense category that is tax free with no limits, so we need to consult the HMRC guides for self employed small traders.

HMRC have a help-sheet, No 222, that explains the various categories of allowable and non-allowable expenses in the tax self assessment form below. Firstly in the financial expenses section this includes 'Repayment of the loans, overdrafts or finance arrangements'. These are not allowable.

Secondly in the section for 'Interest on bank, other business loans and alternative finance payments' what IS ALLOWED (for cash basis users) is the interest up to a maximum amount you can claim of £500.

[Note: Our view, and many accountants agree, is that clearly PayPal and eBay fees are not interest on loans and so do not belong in box 17 of the tax self assessment form above and so are not classed as 'Interest Payable' on the Simplex 'Payments other than for Stock' Form. If you put them in the Interest section then there is a danger that once they total over £500 you pay more tax. Please note that this book gives you information but is not formal tax or accounting or bookkeeping or financial advice.]

The best tax free treatment of the PayPal fees and eBay final value fees is to think of them as fees that are associated with a sale. They are a 'cost of a sale'. An eBay fee is like a sales commission which is an allowable expense according to the HMRC notes to the Self Assessment form SA103F. You cannot make a sale without these two fees and if you do not make a sale then you do not pay them. The best category then is 'Cost of Sales' and this belongs in the 'Payments for Business Stock' Simplex style Form below, along with the payment for stock.

Payments for Business Stock			
Date or Chq No	To whom paid	Cash Col 9	Cheques, credit and debit cards Col 10

Simplex Style Payments for Business Stock

PayPal Fees - PayPal statement reconciliation

As we know we must pin down any payments to the exact transaction using the related source documents. In the case of PayPal fees we have seen that the PayPal do not send an invoice. They simply take the fee for each transaction from the gross money the customer pays through PayPal.

We are interested to find out if the payments by customers this week have all had the fee deducted. We can find out by examining the last week of the PayPal statement below:

Date	Time	Time Z	Name	Type	Status	Curre	Gross	Fee	From	To Em	Trans
30-04-2	12:45:00	BST	STEPHEN	PayPa	Comp	GBP	60	-2.24	STEVEE29@	4VV66	
29-04-2	11:45:00	BST	ALAN AVE	PayPa	Comp	GBP	74.6	-2.34	ALanA	lbrow	8HRD9
28-04-2	21:55:00	BST	PETER AL!	PayPa	Comp	GBP	74.6	-2.34	PandE	lbrow	6BJl12
28-04-2	11:55:00	BST	MATT LEE	PayPa	Comp	GBP	74.6	-2.34	MLEE:	lbrow	5GGl4
28-04-2	20:14:52	BST	Bank Acc(	Withd	Comp	GBP	-560	0			4U810
28-04-2	17:55:00	BST	DAN KNO	PayPa	Comp	GBP	74.6	-2.34	DKNO	lbrow	6SJU3
28-04-2	9:55:00	BST	CARL PEA	PayPa	Comp	GBP	74.6	-2.34	CP123	lbrow	6ugc2
27-04-2	11:55:00	BST	CONNOR	PayPa	Comp	GBP	74.6	-2.34	CCCCr	lbrow	4AGU:
25-04-2	9:17:15	BST	KEITH BAI	PayPa	Comp	GBP	74.6	-2.34	kb123	lbrow	3R050
25-04-2	10:50:45	BST	CARL LYM	PayPa	Comp	GBP	74.6	-2.34	Calrar	lbrow	2CY34
25-04-2	22:52:23	BST	NICHOLA!	PayPa	Comp	GBP	74.6	-2.34	NBB@	lbrow	4CX34
25-04-2	23:55:00	BST	FRANK W	PayPa	Comp	GBP	74.6	-2.34	Frankl	lbrow	3CFY3
24-04-2	9:31:40	BST	ADAM SN	PayPa	Comp	GBP	74.6	-2.34	adam:	lbrow	7MF9:
23-04-2	10:31:40	BST	FRANCES	PayPa	Comp	GBP	74.6	-2.34	fpoole	lbrow	7MF9:
22-04-2	11:31:40	BST	SID JAME:	PayPa	Comp	GBP	74.6	-2.34	sbJam	lbrow	7MF9:
21-04-2	12:31:40	BST	PAUL MIL	PayPa	Comp	GBP	74.6	-2.34	Pjmille	lbrow	7MF9:
20-04-2	13:31:40	BST	SCOTT JO	PayPa	Comp	GBP	74.6	-2.34	scottie	lbrow	7MF9:
19-04-2	14:31:40	BST	LINUS PAI	PayPa	Comp	GBP	74.6	-2.34	lpauli:	lbrow	7MF9:
19-04-2	15:31:40	BST	GERRY RC	PayPa	Comp	GBP	74.6	-2.34	grolan	lbrow	7MF9:
17-04-2	11:55:00	BST	eBay	PayPa	Comp	GBP	-102.05	0			34F32

Now we can examine the PayPal statement for the customer sales invoices that we have issued for this week and see that starting with Adam Smith, where we sent him Sales Invoice No 0125, we were paid the full gross sales value of £74.60 and then PayPal deducted a fee of £2.34.

We can check the rest of the payments for PayPal fees against sales invoices this week from No 0126 to No 0136 and tie up each one with a gross income and a PayPal fee, including Stephen Hill who only paid £60 for his shoes and PayPal then only deducted £2.24 in fees.

There are 12 PayPal Fee Merchant Handling deductions by PayPal of which 11 are for £2.34 and one for £2.24. Louise adds these up and then can put the total PayPal merchanting services fee for this week's transactions of £27.98 into her Cash Book as Cost of Sales. Louise can now stamp a copy of the PayPal fees statement PAID and add the date when the last fees were paid on 30/04/20XX and file it in date paid order at the back of her Purchase Invoices 20XX Lever Arch File.

Of course, as with all statement reconciliation, this is a check on the extent to which bills have been received and paid. If Louise had an extra sales invoice that did not show up with a PayPal fee and the Gross Income then she would need to find out why the payment of income and the fee deduction was missing. Equally if she had a PayPal line with some income but she had not got the Sales Invoice then she would need to print out another copy for her files. Missing Sales Invoices are viewed with suspicion by HMRC.

Her Cash Book form 'Payments for Business Stock' now looks like this.

\multicolumn{4}{c}{Payments for Business Stock}			
Date or Chq No	To whom paid	Cash Col 9	Cheques, credit and debit cards Col 10
25/04/20XX	Spanish Shoes	417 60	
30/04/20XX	Cost of Sales PayPal Fees - March 20XX	27 98	

Simplex Style Payments for Business Stock

Ebay Final Value Fees

This eBay invoice below for March 20XX was automatically paid by PayPal in April and April is when eBay email Louise with the link to the invoice. So although the bill is partly for March she enters it into her books in April.

Invoice number
083115-79019712345

INVOICE
31 March 20XX

Account summary   01 March – 31 March Pacific Time
New fees Includes promotional savings and United Kingdom VAT at the applicable rate.
BasicBusiness Shop Advance Monthly Subscription for April 20XX £19.99
Final value fees £82.06
Subtotal £102.05
Total due £102.05
Do you have a question about the total amount due? We're help!
You have set up an automatic payment method. Your invoice amount will be automatically deducted from your account between 15 April 20XX and 17 April 20XX.
account between 15 April 20XX and 17 April 20XX.
The amount deducted may vary based on recent payments or credits.
Make a onetime payment
Change your payment details
Promotional savings (View details)
Insertion fees-£0.00
Advanced listing upgrade fees-£0.00
Total Saved**-£0.00

**Total saved is an estimate and may not include all promotions credits or reflect changes in your eligibility for promotions

We have already made the Cash Book entry for the advertising fees of £19.99 for April, but we have not entered the eBay 'Final Value Fees' which is the other part of this purchase invoice, which total £82.06 for April.

Once again, as we mentioned with the PayPal fees there is a danger we will pay more tax is we treat these eBay commissions on sales as financial charges.
Since they are fees associated with sales and are a cost of those sales we enter these, in the same way as PayPal fees into the Cash Book form 'Payment for Business Stock' as a Cost of Sales.

Our Cash Book form now looks like this:

Payments for Business Stock					
Date or Chq No	To whom paid	Cash Col 9		Cheques, credit and debit cards Col 10	
25/04/20XX	Spanish Shoes	417	60		
15/04/20XX	Cost of Sales PayPal Fees - April 20XX	27	98		
30/04/20XX	Cost of Sales Ebay Fees - March 20XX	82	06		

Simplex Style Payments for Business Stock

Chapter Eight – Finalising the Simplex Style Postings

What you will find in this section

- ✓ Credit Card Statement
- ✓ Postage
- ✓ Car/Van Allowance
- ✓ Home Use Allowance
- ✓ Simplex Bookkeeping Summary
- ✓ Filing Systems Explained

In this next part we move on to the final straight as far as bookkeeping using a Simplex style of Analysed Cash Book is concerned. The bank statement below only has a payment to the credit card company to consider as an expense and we will consider the PayPal Transfer of £560 in the section about transfers.

Later we will also examine some expenses that do not show up anywhere as payments on either the bank statement or the PayPal statement. These are car/van costs and home use costs. The treatment of these in the books is also explained later in this section.

Credit Card Statement

The item of £72.60 paid on 30/04/20XX to the credit card company on the bank statement below can now be posted into our cash book form once we have checked what it was for with some source documents as usual.

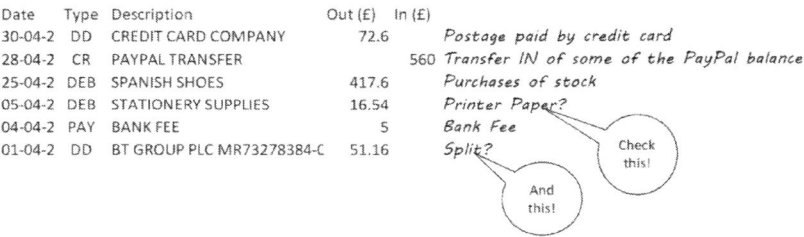

We need to consult the source document of the credit card statement below. Here we can see that the £72.60 was the total amount accumulated, and paid off on 30/04/20XX, after the payment for 11 items to be posted were paid by the credit card at the post office.

Credit Card Statement

Transaction	Posting Date	Billing	Merchant	Mercl	Mercl	Mercl	Reference Nur	Del	SICMCC
30-04-20XX	30-04-20XX	£72.60	DIRECT DEB	THANK YOU				C	0
29-04-20XX	29-04-20XX	£6.60	POST OFF	WIRR/	GBR	CH49	5.53778E+22	D	5542
29-04-20XX	29-04-20XX	£6.60	POST OFF	WIRR/	GBR	CH49	5.53778E+22	D	5542
28-04-20XX	28-04-20XX	£6.60	POST OFF	WIRR/	GBR	CH49	5.53778E+22	D	5542
28-04-20XX	28-04-20XX	£6.60	POST OFF	WIRR/	GBR	CH49	5.53778E+22	D	5542
28-04-20XX	28-04-20XX	£6.60	POST OFF	WIRR/	GBR	CH49	5.53778E+22	D	5542
27-04-20XX	27-04-20XX	£6.60	POST OFF	WIRR/	GBR	CH49	5.53778E+22	D	5542
25-04-20XX	25-04-20XX	£6.60	POST OFF	WIRR/	GBR	CH49	5.53778E+22	D	5542
25-04-20XX	25-04-20XX	£6.60	POST OFF	WIRR/	GBR	CH49	5.53778E+22	D	5542
25-04-20XX	25-04-20XX	£6.60	POST OFF	WIRR/	GBR	CH49	5.53778E+22	D	5542
25-04-20XX	25-04-20XX	£6.60	POST OFF	WIRR/	GBR	CH49	5.53778E+22	D	5542
24-04-20XX	24-04-20XX	£6.60	POST OFF	WIRR/	GBR	CH49	5.53778E+22	D	5542

Are these business items?

Postage

But were all 11 items business items of postage? We need to consult another set of source documents – the post office till receipts, which Louise has in her weekly folder, one of which is shown below:

Here we can see that there a till receipt that matches a payment on 28/04/20XX for the £6.60 on the credit card statement. There is a reference on the till receipt to the postcode OX5 2QD. This is the postcode of the customer Adam Smith from Oxfordshire who received the goods on invoice no 0125. This can be checked by referring to the filed Sales Invoices.

Louise can check through each of the Post Office Till receipts to find out which customer they were for and she does this by matching them with the Post Codes on the Sales Invoices that are in her Sales Invoices Lever Arch File.

She normally pays for the postage one at a time in order to get the proof of postage with the post code for each item. She uses her personal credit card here which she has started using recently and she uses it ONLY to pay for postage. You can access this statement and all the post office till receipts via the Appendix link address.

The credit card statement indeed shows the last 11 items of postage that match the sales invoices 0125 to 0135 and the till receipts' postcodes. Note that Louise also sold a 12th pair of shoes to a relative that were collected from her home and did not incur a postage cost.

Now that Louise can match the bank statement payment of £72.60 to the credit card company and it is all for business postage expense she can enter that amount for postage into her Simplex Cash Book Form for 'Payments other than for Stock' and tick the item off on her bank statement and file the post office receipts and credit card statement as PAID invoices in her Purchase Invoices 20XX Lever Arch File.

Louise can also check if there are till receipts she has in her weekly document folder that are missing from the credit card statement lines which may need to be carried over to next month.

The use of a credit card makes for less bank fee payments on her shared bank current account since there is only one entry when the credit card balance is paid off by the bank by direct debit. However it does introduce the complication of needing to check that the items on the credit card statement are all for business use and this means checking each of the post office till receipts and the sales invoices.

Car and Home Use Allowances

We have not yet sorted out what to do about the house and car allowances, so we cannot yet add up the Cash Book form of 'Payments other than for Stock'.

As we have suggested earlier in this book the self-employed eBay trader can take advantage of the 'Simplified Expenses' HMRC tax methods. In effect this means that there is a rate for car miles and a rate for house use.

The problem then arises about what to do about the cost as an expense. Obviously there are no invoices for petrol or car repairs, so there is nothing to file in our Purchase Invoices 20XX Lever Arch File to record as being paid.

You cannot really afford to ignore these car expenses since if you went 10,000 miles in the year on business then you would be missing £4500 in expenses and then be overstating your profits in your accounts and paying for the car use yourself. This could also lead to you overpaying income tax and national insurance.

The best way to work out your profit, and then know what your correct tax and national insurance is going to be, is to charge the accounts with the car or van allowances as you go along so that you do not get a surprise at the end of the tax year.

The last week in the month is the best time to post these allowances since by then you know the home use hours and the monthly miles driven wholly on business.

Car Mileage Allowance

The first 10,000 miles each year of 'wholly and exclusively' business miles have an allowance of 45p per mile. Any further miles have an allowance of 25p (in 2016).

The recommended way to get these allowances right is to have a Guildhall type of mileage log book.

These are available from Amazon and you just keep it in the car and fill it in for every journey in your vehicle with the start and finish ROUND TRIP odometer readings, journey mileage and which type of journey it is - personal or business. Then every month simply add up the business miles. Keep your book in the car until the end of the tax year and then put it in your 20XX box file.

Louise uses the mileage log book which she totals on to an A4 sheet of paper for her purchase invoices files and this month her business miles to the post office totalled 120 miles. She now can charge the 120 x 0.45 = £54 to the Simplex Cash Book. Louise adds a new line in the Payments other than for Stock Simplex form in the last week of this month. She can file the A4 mileage total log in her Purchase Invoices 20XX Lever Arch File once it is marked PAID. She keeps her mileage log book in the car at all times.

We should just mention that since the car mileage rates vary depending on annual mileage, Louise must check at the end of the year that she has not exceeded 10,000 miles on business, since any miles over than will be at the lower rate of 25p per mile (2016).

Home Office Use Allowance

As we have mentioned earlier in this book, the self-employed trader who opts for the new 'Simplified Expenses' tax rules does not then need to keep bills for rent, or heat and power or insurance and cleaning.

The 'Simplified Expenses' tax allowance for these costs is based simply on the basis of how many hours are spent at home each month working for the business.

Again there is a need for some data collection by the trader. Louise has purchased a cheap diary she keeps just for the purpose of recording her eBay business working at home hours. Every day she records when she starts work for the business and when she finishes. She also notes the times that customers or suppliers ring her up and how long she spends dealing with these queries. She also notes how much time she spends doing her accounts filing and bookkeeping. At the end of the year she proposes to file her diary in her 20XX box file.

This month Louise has recorded a total of 48 hours working from home in her business so she charges £10 to the accounts for this month entering that into the Cash Book in the 'Payments other than for Stock' form.

The workings from home allowances start at 25 hours per month and have these rates (2016):
Hours of business use per month = 25 - 50 : Flat rate per month = £10
Hours of business use per month = 51 - 100 : Flat rate per month = £18
Hours of business use per month = 101 : Flat rate per month = £26

Note: Although the term working from home seems to apply to you as a trader since it depends on your hours of working on your business matters at home, the allowance is for the use of your home and not for the use of your own time.

You may wonder how you get compensation for your own time. What about your time spent taking the parcels to the post office?

Remember that your time is paid for by your business profits, so note that time in the car is not an allowable expense. It is not hours using your home and its rent, rates, insurance, etc.

The working from home allowance that gives you an increase in your tax free profits from the allowable expense of £10 a month for using your spare bedroom in your house may not seem much when you spend 1 or 2 hours a day in there sorting out your web auctions, packing and sorting out customer problems. You could decide that your rent, heating, lighting, insurance and rates for one of your rooms must be worth more than that.

You can opt to not use the allowance system and work out the share that the spare bedroom uses based on the square feet of the room compared to the square feet of the whole house. Remember that you will then have to collect all the bills for rent, heating, lighting, insurance and rates every month and spend time filing them as with Purchase Invoices and entering the split amounts between personal and business each month.

Louise has now completed her bookkeeping entries for all her purchase invoices and she can mark all the invoices as PAID with the actual date paid, and move them to the back of her Purchase Invoice 20XX Lever arch file. She can file the month's bank and PayPal statements in her box file.

With all the Simplex Cash Book entries processed, Louise can add up her Simplex style form for 'Payments other than for Stock' below and move the totals from all her weekly Simplex style forms for each sub category of expense and purchase to the summary pages at the rear of her Simplex Book. At the end of the year she can then fill in her tax form.

Simplex Book Page Weekly Layout Style
Last Week in May 20XX

Payments other than for Stock				
Nature of Payment	Cash Col 11		Cheques, credit and debit cards Col 12	
Employment Cost (i) Wages				
(ii) Inland Revenue PAYE &NI				
Premises Cost (i) Rent and Rates				
(ii) Light, Heat and Insurance				
(iii) Cleaning				
Repairs				
Gen.Admin. (i) Telephone	12	07		
(ii) Postage	72	60		
(iii) Stationery, etc.	16	54		
Motor Expenses (i) Fuel				
(ii) Servicing & Repairs, etc				
Travel & Subsistence				
Advertising & Entertainment	19	99		
Legal and Professional				
Interest Payable				
Other Expenses				
Lottery Prizes Paid				
Scratch Cards Prizes Paid				
Bank Fees	1	00		
Car Mileage Allowance May 120 miles x 0.45	54	00		
Working from home allowance May 50 hours	10	00		
	186	20		

You do not have the back of the book sheets since we are only practising on one week.

We now perhaps need to explain where our excess money is, if we have any, after we have paid for all our expenses.

Transfers

We have worked our way through the current account bank statement and found that the PayPal transfer of £560 was carried out by Louise towards the end of the month so that some of the net sales income could be used to pay for future expenses.

This is not really a transaction as far as our business bookkeeping is concerned since it is not money in or out but a transfer from one business related account - our PayPal account - to another business related account - our shared personal/business bank current account.

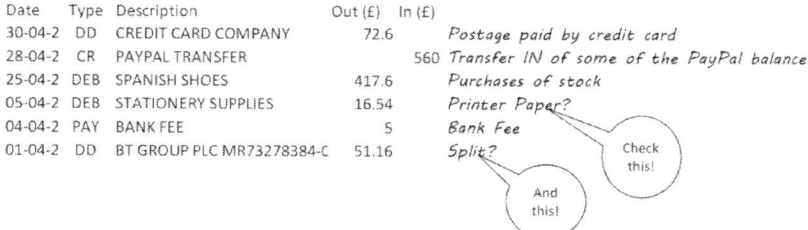

Date	Type	Description	Out (£)	In (£)	
30-04-2	DD	CREDIT CARD COMPANY	72.6		Postage paid by credit card
28-04-2	CR	PAYPAL TRANSFER		560	Transfer IN of some of the PayPal balance
25-04-2	DEB	SPANISH SHOES	417.6		Purchases of stock
05-04-2	DEB	STATIONERY SUPPLIES	16.54		Printer Paper?
04-04-2	PAY	BANK FEE	5		Bank Fee
01-04-2	DD	BT GROUP PLC MR73278384-C	51.16		Split? Check this! And this!

Eventually Louise will take some money out of the business as her profits which she will spend on personal items or put into a savings account. When this happens she can make a posting or proprietor's drawings in her books. What she does with her excess business money will have no impact on her business profit.

Or she may leave it in the business and invest it in a wider range of products. Either way there is no real separation between the money in the business and her personal money and 'the books' will continue to just reflect the transactions of the business and be used to complete her tax return. The business 'books' are not concerned with Louise's personal money but the business affects her. If the business makes a loss, then the loss belongs to Louise personally as a self employed sole trader.

Cash or Cheques Income Payments

We have concentrated on an eBay trader who gets paid by PayPal. If you are not an eBay trader you can still use the bookkeeping methods described in this book. The only difference is that when the money comes in by cash the money needs to be paid in to the bank and the 'lodgement slip' that the bank issue, recording the cash in, should then be filed too in the box file. If you have paid for a business only bank account you will be given a paying in book and will need to keep the stubs in the box file.

Congratulations!!

Well done for getting to here. You now know how to 'do the books' and 'do the filing' (if you have read the filing section next chapter) using a simple Cash Book type of bookkeeping system. Whilst that may well be enough for your business if is it is small and has limited transactions each week, you could stop here. But you may wish to get into a bit more technology and we will start with a specially designed spreadsheet for you that will save you time and then move on to a Cloud based system – QuickBooks Self-Employed.

But first here is a summary of what you have learnt so far and some comments about the Simplex type of system and how it compares to a spreadsheet or Cloud system.

Bookkeeping and Simplex Training

These first sections have shown you that single entry cash basis bookkeeping is fairly simple. You have learned how money in and out of the sole trader business can be tracked through bank and PayPal statements and that supporting source documents can enable you to then categorise the transactions for the Analysed Cash Book. You have seen that a good filing system is needed to keep records for the tax man/woman for 6 years.

You have followed the Case Study through a typical trading week and seen how to 'do the books' and 'do the filing' using the Simplex style of cash book and several Lever Arch Files, folders and boxes. Look at the filing chapter if you have not done that training yet.

You could now use the Simplex system to do your own books and to submit your tax return at the end of the financial year. The HMRC registration process and completion of the self assessment form is covered in the Taxes section at the end of the book.

What to do next

If you are reading this book for interest and to further your knowledge then you should carry on to learn how technology is changing bookkeeping for the self employed.

If you have started an new trading business and have not yet started on your accounts then you should try the provided blank Simplex forms for your own business and work through your own bank and PayPal statements and start to use your supporting business documents - Invoices - to enter money in and money out transactions into the Cash Book forms. Try bookkeeping posting for a week of trading to see if your think that it is worth buying a Simplex hardback book and a filing system set of Lever Arch Files, Document Folder and Document Box or indeed worth moving on to newer technologies now you understand single entry bookkeeping.

Simplex Review

Simplex has been quite easy to follow using the forms supplied in this book, but the categories do not reflect the 'Simplified Expenses Tax' system rules for home and car allowances. However you can add lines categories yourself

The Simplex Book is nice if you like to do your own adding up and prefer a piece of paper to a spreadsheet

A self employed sole trader sharing a personal bank account with the business will not be able to use the bank balance forms on the weekly page, since the monies in are coming to the account and the monies out are going from a regular shared bank current account with personal transactions; so no matching of bank statement balances with those tracked in the Cash Book is possible.

Simplex lacks any instant category analysis that you can have with more up to date systems such as Analysed Cash Book Spreadsheets and Cloud Based Computer Bookkeeping packages like QuickBooks Self-Employed

Simplex does not work out your profit (excess of income over expenses) until you add everything up at the end of the year

Simplex does not tell you what your tax and National Insurance will be

You cannot import your bank statement into a Simplex Cash Book

But a cheap and easy system for the first time self-employed trader who sells less than £200 a week

This kit also provides a link to a free Simplex set of blank forms via the Appendix link. In the next section we will try and understand how the paperwork documents that a business accumulates is dealt with correctly.

We will start by examining how to deal with and correctly file the paperwork documents associated with money going out of the business. This is slightly boring but necessary. A good bookkeeping filing system is essential in case your business is selected for examination by HMRC. You do not want the tax man/woman to fine you due to not having the right records for your business.

Chapter Nine – Filing Systems

Before we examine the impact of new technology on bookkeeping we are going to learn about the role of document filing in some detail and explore the steps that are essential to good bookkeeping.

You will need a good record filing system to do your own bookkeeping. This will save you time and money in the end and is well worth the effort. Finding that you are missing a record of some money you spent for the business and not finding out until months later will be costly since that cost then cannot be claimed as a reduction in your tax without an adequate record of the spending. So keep your records up to date using the system we suggest here.

The flow chart below shows the steps for Louise in the movement of information and order for filing of supporting source documents that together are the evidence of money going out of the business.

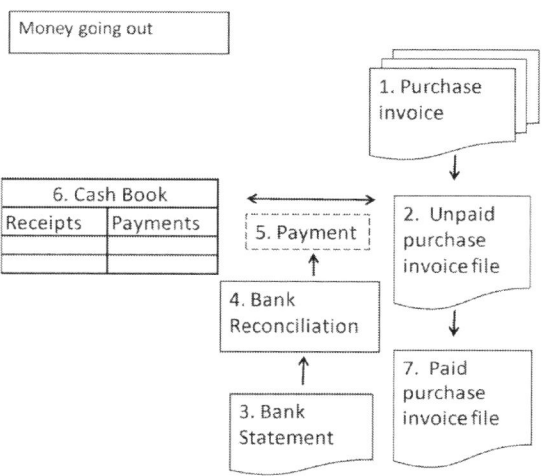

Money Going Out Process Flow – Paperwork Filing

The numbered steps in the chart are explained below:

1. Purchase Invoice

A purchase invoice record of a business purchase is the starting point for the business source document filing process. An example would be where Louise orders some business stock from her wholesaler. The wholesaler will then send an invoice that usually shows the following information.

- A unique identification Invoice number
- Date of invoice

- Customer billing Name
- Customer billing Address
- Delivery Address
- Item clear Description
- Amount being charged
- The supplier Business Name
- The supplier Business Address
- The Total Amount Owed
- The supplier contact details

Louise puts the same list of information on her own Sales Invoices, which we will come to later.

Louise has a Purchase Invoice example below from her wholesaler - Spanish Shoes - in her folder where she collects her business paperwork each week.

Spanish Shoes   Invoice

Invoice To:
Mrs. L. Brown

Businessshoes
3 St Georges
Grove
Greasby
Wirral
Merseyside
CH46 6DD
UK
Phone
Customer ID

Delivery Address:
Mrs. L. Brown

Businessshoes
3 St Georges
Grove
Greasby
Wirral
Merseyside
CH46 6DD
UK
Phone
Customer ID

Date: 25/04/20XX
Customer #: 7804
Invoice #: 0420
Terms: Cash Account

Qty	Item No	Description	Unit Price £	Total £
4	P14001/09	Mens Derby Lace Up Black Size 9	29.00	116.00
4	P12001/10	Mens Oxford Lace Up Black Size 10	29.00	116.00
4	P14001/11	Mens Derby Lace Up Black Size 11	29.00	116.00
			Subtotal	348.00
			VAT	69.60
			Total	£ 417.60

Make all cheques payable to Spanishshoes
Thank you for your business!

Spanish Shoes Ltd, Seven Acres Business Park, Woodbridge IP12 4PS, UK

2.   Unpaid section of the Purchase Invoices 20XX Lever Arch File.

Louise has a large lever arch file labelled Purchase Invoices 20XX. At the front of a cardboard divider is where she keeps her UNPAID purchase invoices IN DATE ORDER with the oldest at the back and the newest at the front. So the first job for Louise is to look at the dates on all her UNPAID purchase invoices in her weekly paperwork document folder and to put them in date order in this lever arch file – awaiting her checking for evidence that they have been paid for and when by the business.

The purchase invoice above is UNPAID (until verified as paid on the bank statement) and dated fairly late in the month – on 25th April 20XX. So it will be placed on top of any earlier dated purchase invoices at the UNPAID front of the divider in the Unpaid section of the Purchase Invoices 20XX Lever Arch File.

The Purchase Invoices 20XX Lever Arch File also has the PAID invoices (or equivalents) at the back of the cardboard divider.
 It should be noted that not every purchase generates an invoice like this one from the wholesaler supplier of shoes. When you buy from a retailer and pay for the goods you get a till receipt instead. But as far as your bookkeeping and filing are concerned till receipts are purchase invoices.

A purchase invoice has the issue date on it and the amount paid. Records of all business purchases are filed in the Purchase Invoices 20XX Lever Arch File.

The purchases supporting source documents with data about the amount and date paid documents can take several formats.

For example a bank statement with bank fees is not an invoice but we will need to take a copy of the bank statement page with the fee on and treat it like a purchase invoice. The bank statements themselves are normally filed in a separate document box, but a copy with the bank fee will be kept with the purchase invoice.

PayPal statements are also like purchase invoices and a copy will be filed in the Purchases Invoices Lever Arch Files since they show the payment (deduction by PayPal) date and amount of PayPal merchant handling fees.

 A small self-employed sole business trader may have several types of purchase invoice formats for receipts and statements that are source documents that they have collected which are associated with running the business, all of which are treated as records of business spending on purchases.

Louise has the following UNPAID (and unprocessed into her Cash Book and Filing system) records of business purchases for the last week in April in her business documents weekly folder or at the front, unpaid section, of her Purchase Invoices Lever Arch File.

A bank statement for a current account showing bank charges and several monies in and out

A purchase invoice from a supplier for purchases of goods for business stock

Eleven till receipts from a post office for postage purchases

One purchase invoice from eBay for what eBay call 'final value fees' and the monthly subscription

One Receipt for stationery – printer paper

Twelve sales invoices she has generated and sent a second copy to customers

A bill for telephone and broadband costs
A credit card statement with entries for postage paid

A PayPal monthly statement showing PayPal transactions and merchant handling charges

(However PayPal do not give you a receipt for their charges - you get a statement instead via the Internet).

She also has a set of blank Simplex style Cash Book forms, which are shown in the Appendix.

You will also be shown each of these items as we work through this learning kit as the transactions are entered into the Cash Book.

Louise also keeps a summary of her business Mileage trips on an A4 sheet and a summary of her diary entries for last week of the hours that she spent working on her new business in her home.

3.   Bank Statement

The next step in the filing and bookkeeping process is for Louise to check that her bank statement has recorded all the payments for the purchases that she has paperwork for in her weekly folder.
 The bank statement shows the payments in date order and who was paid and the amount; so she can begin the 'reconciliation' between the bank statement and her invoices.

4.   Bank Reconciliation

The 'Bank Reconciliation' step is basically one of checking the amounts and who was paid on the bank statement, and matching these invoices and other records of purchases.

Reconciliation of larger businesses and registered Limited companies with more complex accounts (that have an independent business bank account) normally involves checks that the business bank statement balance match (at the end of the week or month) with the business money bank cash balance recorded in the books

However as a shared personal and business self-employed trader we can only do the checking of the money in and money out against the transactions documents. This is because the business money in and out of the bank account is shared with personal spending, so the bank balance will not tally with the balance of the business money worked out from the last bank statement balance and the business records.

The other reason we cannot reconcile the bank balance with the accounts analysis is that the money in to the business bank account comes through a PayPal account and will stay there unless moved by the account holder into the bank current account.

Nevertheless we can carry out the steps of checking the bank statement entries against our invoices and other records of money movement in order to reconcile our books.

This step of reconciliation of each of the bank statement lines with specific purchase records will also highlight where a purchase invoice remains unpaid – and cannot be entered into the Cash Book yet as paid.

It would also highlight where a payment has been made on the bank statement but the purchase record is missing.

IT IS THEREFORE VITAL THAT EVERY PURCHASE, HOWEVER SMALL, HAS A PURCHASE RECORD!

5.   Payment

If a specific Purchase Invoice record (or Purchase record such as a till receipt) amount and who has been paid can be matched with a specific bank statement line then that bank statement line now verifies the payment and the bank statement line can now be ticked off and the Purchase Invoice updated to PAID status and annotated with the date that the bank statement paid the amount.

Louise has a multi-function pre-inked stamp she uses for the purpose of marking the purchase record as PAID with the date paid. Without a stamp Louise would simply write PAID and the date paid on the invoice.

6.   Cash Book Entry

Next Louise can now enter the details of each purchase into her Simplex Cash Book under the relevant expense category heading.

7.   Paid Purchase Invoice File

Louise can move any invoice or purchase record that she has checked off and stamped as paid into the back of her Purchase Invoices 20XX Lever Arch file and keep them IN DATE PAID ORDER with the oldest at the rear and the newest at the front, all behind the cardboard divider.

Money Coming In Process Flow – Paperwork Filing

As with money out, there is a similar set of process steps for money coming in to the business from sales. It is less complex in terms of collecting the paperwork evidence of money in since Louise generates all her own Sales Invoices as the example below. The same sort of steps apply so there is a Sales Invoice 20XX Lever Arch file that has PAID invoices at the back of a cardboard divider and UNPAID invoices in front of the divider.

There is a MAJOR difference in the ORDER of the filing of PAID invoices

The Sales Invoices each have a unique Sales Invoice Number and they are filed in the Sales Invoices Lever Arch File 20XX in INVOICE NUMBER ORDER with the lowest number at the rear.

This is an important part of the checking system since once verified as paid the back of the cardboard divider should contain a full and complete set of consecutive invoices as far as the invoice numbers are concerned.

						Invoice
Businessshoes				Date:		24th April
Be Smart and Comfortable				Invoice #:		0125
				Customer ID:		C0125

To:	Adam Smith	Ship to:	Adam Smith	
	15 Oxford Rd		15 Oxford Rd	
	Hampton Poyle		Hampton Poyle	PAID
	Kidlington		Kidlington	
	Oxfordshire		Oxfordshire	
	OX5 2QD		OX5 2QD	

Salesperson	Shipping Method	Shipping Terms	Delivery Date	Payment Terms	Due Date
Louise	Next Day signed for	Free Postage	25th April 20XX	Paypal	Paid

Qty	Item #	Description	Unit Price	Discount	Line Total
1.00	OX001/9/B	Oxford Size 9 Black	£ 74.60		£ 74.60

Total Discount

Subtotal £ 74.60
Sales Tax
Total £ **74.60**
Total Owed 0.00

Make all payments via Paypal to this email address: lbrown1947@outlook.com

3 St Georges Grove, Greasby, Wirral, Merseyside CH46 6DD, UK

Here we can see that the invoice dated 24th April 20XX is Invoice Number 0125. We expect this, when marked as Paid, to be in front of Sales Invoice 0124 at the back of the Sales Invoice 20XX Lever Arch File.

You may be wondering what to do if you make a mistake on an invoice or get a customer return or sell an item privately. An error in a Sales Invoice should still create an invoice and it should still be put in the right order at the back of the Sales Invoices 20XX Lever Arch File and marked as VOID. The same goes for a return which can be marked as a RETURN. The informal sale should also generate a Sales Invoice. HMRC will see missing sales invoice numbers as suspicious.

There is a short video about keeping records from HMRC here:

https://www.youtube.com/watch?v=WYUhtUQL0Q0

There are no O's in this just number 0.

Now that both basic bookkeeping using a Simplex style cash book has been covered and you know how to do filing of documents we can look at new technology and spreadsheets.

Chapter Ten – New Technology – Spreadsheets

Part Two

> **What you will find in this section**
>
> ✓ **Analysed Cash Book Spreadsheet**
>
> ✓ **QuickBooks Self-Employed**
>
> ✓ **Break-Even Point**
>
> ✓ **Taxes**
>
> ✓ **Download a PayPal Statement**
>
> ✓ **Appendix Materials and Links**

This section will show you how new technologies can make life easier when managing your bookkeeping.

Computer based ready formatted Bookkeeping Spreadsheets save time by taking over the job of adding up and analysing your expense categories and providing faster data entry.

Even faster data entry can be achieved through the direct connection of your bank and PayPal statements to your Cash Book using the QuickBooks Self-Employed computer package which you can try for free

Or you can import the bank statements to your laptop and read the file into the same system. QuickBooks also lets you manage your invoice filing through the use of Cloud storage of photos of the invoices.

Both spreadsheets and QuickBooks Self-Employed keep track of your profit after every bookkeeping posting.

Knowing when and how your business makes a profit is a key task for every business owner and we show you how to work out how you make a profit and the effect of changes of selling volumes, selling prices or costs.

We complete the book with a section on how to complete your tax return.

What is an Analysed Cash Book?

The technology has moved on from books with pages of formatted forms per week. An Analysed Cash Book Spreadsheet is a cash book with columns for each expense type. You can download one especially designed for the sole trader and this kit via the Appendix link.

Is a Simplex Book an Analysed Cash Book? Yes since the Simplex Book has pre-formatted boxes where you post transaction details.
You will recall that the Simplex Cash Book kept track each week of types of income and expenditure and that the weekly totals for each category of for example for 'Payments other than for Stock' are transferred week by week to an annual total set of pages.

This means that at the end of the year, and week by week, you can see the amount spent in a particular category such as Postage, summarised at the back of a Simplex Cash Book. In other words the breakdown of the various categories of expenses has been 'analysed'.

Obviously there is quite a lot of manual transferring of figures in the Simplex system from the lines in each category each week to the lines in the summary at the back of the book.

You might make mistakes transferring totals from the weekly sub categories to the sub categories at the back of the book. You also might make mistakes adding up the quarterly and annual figures in a Simplex Book. The addition of an extra zero can play havoc! Because you cannot carry out Cash balance bank reconciliation each week you may not notice any mistakes.

Technology has moved on so that now Simplex formatted form styles can be put in a spreadsheet. In fact you can create your own quite easily if you know how to use a spreadsheet. Make a weekly set of Simplex style forms and then copy that page another 51 times into new worksheets for a year book. But it will lack any ongoing totalling of expense categories, unless you make some connections between weekly sheets yourself

Free Analysed Cash Book Spreadsheet

The analysed Cash Book Spreadsheet available free with this kit, has done all the hard work for you and added the ability to automatically update category totals each time you add a transaction.

And the other great thing about this type of free spreadsheet is that it already has the categories names available for you when you post a transaction in a drop down box.

Date	Supplier name	Detail of supply	Ref	Amount	Payment Method	Expense Detail
05/05/20XX	Spanish Shoes	Oxford Black Shoes	03261	252.00	Personal bank	

1. Enter the usual details

2. Choose the Category from the drop down box

Expense Detail options:
- Advertising and PR
- Bank and PayPal charges
- Commissions payable to Ebay
- Employer's NI
- Equipment expensed
- Motor expenses
- Other expenses

Here we can see that when entering a Purchase Invoice into the spreadsheet, it has a drop down dialogue box with options to choose as in the picture above. This saves time typing in the name of a type of expense. In addition the amount paid that you have put in, associated with that drop down category is then automatically added up for you every time you enter an amount for that category.

If you have a web connected PC or laptop why not have a go with the downloaded spreadsheet from the Appendix link yourself as we go along to see how easy it is?

If you do not have a copy of Microsoft Office Excel you can get the free Open Office suite via an Appendix link address to run on your laptop or PC computer at home.

Case Study Bookkeeping with the Analysed Cash Book Spreadsheet

Louise starts her use of the spreadsheet like the one you can download in the same way as posting and filing transactions in a Simplex Cash Book using a paper and a pencil system. She starts with her joint personal/ business current account bank statement, narrowed down into just the business elements as shown below.

Date	Type	Description	Out (£)	In (£)	
30-04-2	DD	CREDIT CARD COMPANY	72.6		*Postage paid by credit card*
28-04-2	CR	PAYPAL TRANSFER		560	*Transfer IN of some of the PayPal balance*
25-04-2	DEB	SPANISH SHOES	417.6		*Purchases of stock*
05-04-2	DEB	STATIONERY SUPPLIES	16.54		*Printer Paper?*
04-04-2	PAY	BANK FEE	5		*Bank Fee*
01-04-2	DD	BT GROUP PLC MR73278384-C	51.16		*Split?*

Check this!

And this!

Louise starts with the Phone Bill. She has already got all her paperwork purchase invoices filed as PAID in her Lever Arch Files. She is not going to mark them as PAID twice since she is just trying out the Analysed Cash Book spreadsheet.

Posting transactions will be a lot faster now that her invoices are all organised, but of course if this spreadsheet was her only system she would have to start with her weekly document folder.

But with her existing filed invoice notes in her Lever Arch Files she can quickly begin to check the bank statement with the Invoice for Phone and Broadband amount paid and date. We recall that this was a split cost since Louise also has personal use for the Internet and phone.

Her notes on the filed phone bill reported: The total split of the £51.16 that belongs to the business is £8.72 + £3.35 = £12.07

She can now try with the spreadsheet. Why don't you try as well?

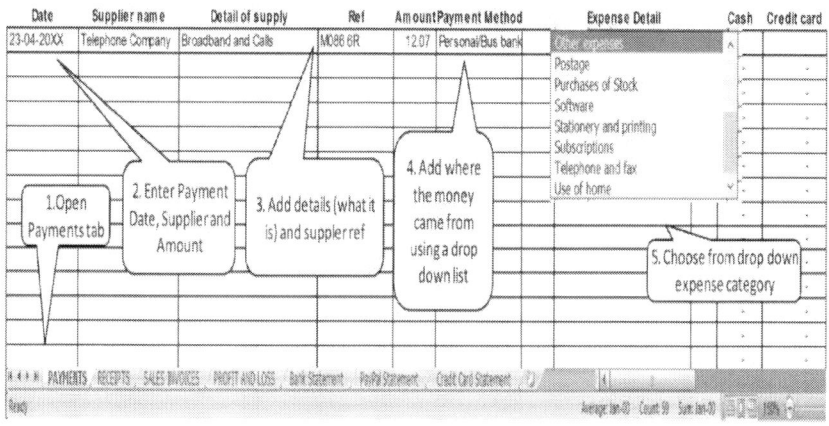

The spreadsheet will open in Microsoft Office Word or in the free Open Office Spreadsheet available via the Appendix link. You should have Open Office or Word installed on your computer before you get the free formatted kit spreadsheet as a download.

The kit spreadsheet is easy to operate in order to post a transaction and the details from the invoice and bank statement into the Cash Book columns.

1.   When the spreadsheet file opens, choose the first worksheet PAYMENTS tab from the selection at the bottom of the sheet.

2.   Now enter the bill/invoice/receipt/statement MINIMUM details of Date, Supplier and Amount. Remember this is the DATE PAID on the bank statement and not the date we are posting the transaction.

3.   You can enter some extra details, an improvement on a Simplex Cash Book. Louise puts in that her first entry of the phone invoice is for Broadband and Calls and add the supplier's reference from the top of the particular telephone bill - of M086 6R. This can be useful if she has various similar bills and makes it easy for HMRC to see she has a good cross-referencing system for her accounts.

4.   There is a drop down list for where the money came from. Louise selects the joint personal/business current account. Credit card, Cash and Other are the remaining options in the drop down list.

5.   Next choose from the drop down list of expense categories and press ENTER or left click your mouse. Also here are income categories.

6.   The power of an integrated spreadsheet is shown here as the columns to the right automatically copy the amount from the latest transaction into each category column and then total it at the bottom of the column. Try and add that bill again on a second line and see for yourself how the category totals are added up automatically.
 What else can the spreadsheet do?

Well switch tabs to the profit/loss worksheet tab and see for yourself.

Impressive!

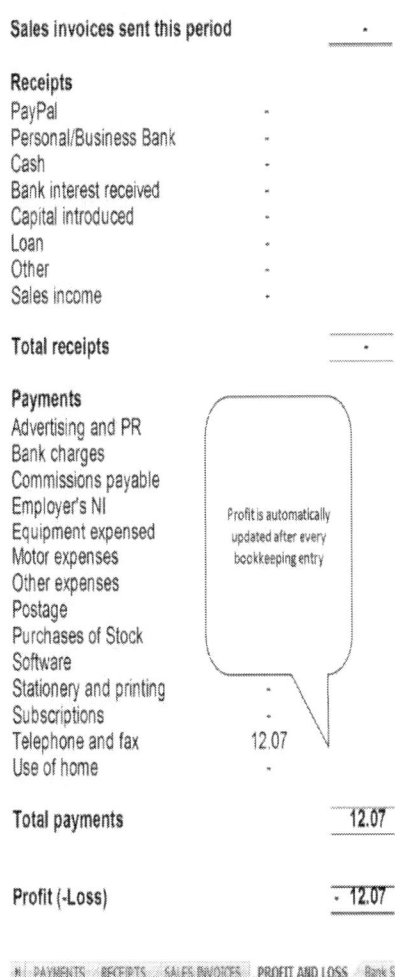

Louise now goes back to the PAYMENTS tab and enters two more postings – the bank fee and stationery, from her filed PURCHASE INVOICES LEVER ARCH FILE – from the paid section – just to see how this compares to the Simplex book.

Date	Supplier name	Detail of supply	Ref	Amount	Payment Method	Expense Detail
23-04-20XX	Telephone Company	Broadband and Ca	M086 6R	12.07	Personal/Bus bank	Telephone and
04-04-20XX	Bank	Monthly Fee April		1.00	Personal/Bus bank	Bank and PayP
15-04-20XX	Staionery Supplier	Printer Paper	DYTMSDRG	16.54	Personal/Bus bank	Stationery and

PAYMENTS RECEIPTS SALES INVOICES PROFIT AND LOSS Bank Statement PayPal Statement Credit Card Statement

The entering or posting takes no time at all and we can easily switch to the Profit view – of course the spreadsheet saves time – but also we know that Louise has already taken time while doing the books with the Simplex forms to sort out the correct payment dates and find the invoices. If she was starting from scratch with her weekly documents file it would take longer.

Purchase of stock was a different set of boxes on the Simplex layout. However this spreadsheet just treats them as purchases, so they go in the PAYMENTS tab section.

Date	Supplier name	Detail of supply	Ref	Amount	Payment Method	Expense Detail
23-04-20XX	Telephone Company	Broadband and Calls	M086 6R	12.07	Personal/Bus	Telephone and fax
04-04-20XX	Bank	Monthly Fee April		1.00	Personal/Bus	Bank and PayPal charges
15-04-20XX	Stationery Supplier	Printer Paper	DYTMSDRGb	16.54	Personal/Bus	Stationery and printing
25-04-20XX	Spanish Shoes	12 Pairs	03261	417.60	Personal/Bus	Purchases of Stock

PAYMENTS RECEIPTS SALES INVOICES PROFIT AND LOSS Bank Statement PayPal Statement Credit Card Statement

We have made the postings for some purchases but what about income from sales?

Invoices and Receipts – No profit until you get paid

In this spreadsheet there is a separation between when we issue a sales invoice and when we get paid for the items. This can be useful if you do not use PayPal and give people credit instead. It is worth just looking at what happens to your self-employed sole trader profit if you send out an invoice and it does not get paid.

Here we enter the single invoice number 0125 using the Sales Invoice Tab on the spreadsheet. We put in when it should be paid – the Due Date. For Louise this should be the date of the 'Buy it Now' eBay sale but the customer may not pay that day.

Date	Customer name	Detail of supply	Invoice no.	Amount	Due date	Date paid	Method
24-04-20XX	Adam Smith	Oxford Size 9 Black	0125	76.40	24-04-20XX	24-04-20XX	PayPal

PAYMENTS | RECEIPTS | SALES INVOICES | PROFIT AND LOSS | Bank Statement | PayPal Statement | Credit Card Statement

Then we look at the Profit tab.

Sales invoices sent this period		76.40
Receipts		
PayPal	-	
Personal/Business Bank	-	
Cash	-	
Bank interest received	-	
Capital introduced	-	
Loan	-	
Other	-	
Sales income	-	
Total receipts		-
Payments		
Advertising and PR	-	
Bank charges	1.00	
Commissions payable	-	
Employer's NI	-	
Equipment expensed	-	
Motor expenses	-	
Other expenses	-	
Postage	-	
Purchases of Stock	417.60	
Software	-	
Stationery and printing	16.54	
Subscriptions	-	
Telephone and fax	12.07	
Use of home	-	
Total payments		447.21
Profit (-Loss)		- 447.21

We can see that issuing an invoice does not give us sales income in 'Total receipts'. In Cash Basis accounting to get that we need to confirm that we have actually been paid and enter into the spreadsheet RECEIPTS TAB and make the posting of the receipt of the payment. We only need the bare details of date, name and amount here since we have the full details in the Sales Invoice Tab entry. Make sure that you also use the Receipt Detail column to categorise the income as Sales Income from the dropdown tabs.

Date	Customer name	Detail of supply	Ref	Amount	Paid to	Receipt Detail
24-04-20XX	Adam Smith			74.60	PayPal	
		Record Money In on the Receipts Tab				

PAYMENTS | RECEIPTS | SALES INVOICES | PROFIT AND LOSS | Bank Statement | PayPal Statement | Credit Card Statement

Now the Profit/Loss Statement below shows some income. Hooray! So make sure that you get paid or you will not have any profit.

Sales invoices sent this period		76.40
Receipts		
PayPal	74.60	
Personal/Business Bank	-	
Cash	-	
Bank interest received	-	
Capital introduced	-	
Loan	-	
Other	-	
Sales income	-	
Total receipts		74.60
Payments		
Advertising and PR	-	
Bank charges	1.00	
Commissions payable	-	
Employer's NI	-	
Equipment expensed	-	
Motor expenses	-	
Other expenses	-	
Postage	-	
Purchases of Stock	417.60	
Software	-	
Stationery and printing	16.54	
Subscriptions	-	
Telephone and fax	12.07	
Use of home	-	
Total payments		447.21
Profit (-Loss)		- 372.61

Now have some try yourself and see if you can complete the spreadsheet postings. You will need to go back to each of the Simplex form postings and step by step repeat the postings for each transaction, using the same source documents.

Remember, if we had not already posted these by practising in the Simplex style forms we would need to go through the process of matching a bank or PayPal entry with the source documents – invoices, till receipts and statements.

Also remember what is essential is the date the money left the business, the name of the supplier and the amount that belongs to the business costs.

Note that eBay Final Value Fees and PayPal fees have been categorised under Purchase of Stock and not bank fees.

Your final sheet payments worksheet should look like this.

Date	Supplier name	Detail of supply	Ref	Amount	Payment Method	Expense Detail
23-04-20XX	Telephone Company	Broadband and Calls	M086 6R	12.07	Personal/Bus bank	Telephone and fax
04-04-20XX	Bank	Monthly Fee April		1.00	Personal/Bus bank	Bank and PayPal charges
15-04-20XX	Stationery Supplier	Printer Paper	DYTMSDR Gb	16.54	Personal/Bus bank	Stationery and printing
25-04-20XX	Spanish Shoes	12 Pairs	03261	417.60	Personal/Bus bank	Purchases of Stock
17-04-20XX	eBay	Subscription Basic	ends 9712345	19.99	Personal/Bus bank	Advertising and PR
17-04-20XX	eBay	Final Value Fees March	ends 9712345	82.06	Personal/Bus bank	Purchases of Stock
30-04-20XX	PayPal Fees	Covers sales 17-30th April	PP Statement	27.98	Personal/Bus bank	Purchases of Stock
30-04-20XX	Postage	Covers 0125 to 0136	CC Statement	72.60	Personal/Bus bank	Postage
30-04-20XX	Car Allowance	April 120 Miles @45p	Mileage Book	54.00	Other	Motor Allowance
30-04-20XX	Home Use Allowance	April 48 Hours	Diary Entries	10.00	Other	Use of home

Some explanations of the completed payment entries are required:

Details of supply tell us something from the invoice or bill about the items.

Ref: Gives us the chance to enter the suppliers unique invoice reference or source of data such as a PayPal (PP) statement.

Payment method. DO NOT BE TEMPTED TO USE 'PAYPAL' OR 'CREDIT CARD' HERE. THE BUSINESS MONEY COMES OUT OF THE BANK JOINT PERSONAL/BUSINESS CURRENT ACCOUNT

NOTE: If you decide to use the Cash Book System with purchases paid on a Credit Card, the money does not leave the business until the credit card is paid off, so whilst the credit card business such as Barclaycard may be the source of funds when paying the supplier, it is not the real source of funds from the business – that is ONLY from the personal/business bank current account.

You may want to use the credit card as a choice of payment for the books, since you know you are going to have to pay off the credit card balance at some time. However if you do use a credit card statement as a source document then and say that this is where the 'money out' happened. Do not then also use the money out of the current account line on the bank statement as a source document.

Payment Method. Where an expenses allowance such as car use has been used there is no cash moving out of the shared personal/business bank account so we use the 'Other 'category of 'payment' to pay the Car or Home Allowance. These then are not cash but are still ALLOWABLE EXPENSE items that REDUCE the tax bill so they need entering into the books.

Expense Details are the choices from the expenses categories drop down boxes.

Your Profit Statement should then look like this:

Sales invoices sent this period		880.60
Receipts		
PayPal	880.60	
Personal/Business Bank	-	
Cash	-	
Bank interest received	-	
Capital introduced	-	
Loan	-	
Other	-	
Sales income	-	
Total receipts		880.60
Payments		
Advertising and PR	19.99	
Bank charges	1.00	
Commissions payable	-	
Employer's NI	-	
Equipment expensed	-	
Motor expenses	54.00	
Other expenses	-	
Postage	72.60	
Purchases of Stock	527.64	
Software	-	
Stationery and printing	16.54	
Subscriptions	-	
Telephone and fax	12.07	
Use of home	10.00	
Total payments		713.84
Profit (-Loss)		166.76

Analysed Cash Book Spreadsheet Summary

The spreadsheet has many advantages over a set of Simplex style forms with a page for a week.

- Adding up automatically saves time and there is less scope for mistakes as there is no transcribing of totals to another page – but you can still make mistakes entering the wrong figures on to a spreadsheet so care is needed! Check figures at least twice.

- Drop down boxes for payment type and expense or income type leads to instant additions in each category and instant analysis of where the money went so far.

- There is still no attempt to balance shared bank account cash balance with the Cash Book Accounts Cash balance. With a shared personal/business bank account for a self-employed trader this is not needed anyway.

- Some free spreadsheets may not reflect the categories of 'Simplified Expenses Tax' system rules for home and car allowances. The one on the link in this kit does.

- Works out your profit as you enter each posting. A real benefit.

- Does not tell you what your tax and National Insurance will be.

- You cannot import your bank or PayPal statement.

- Tracking of Sales Invoices is separate from getting paid – Receipts. Helps to know when you have not been paid, but adds some extra work

- But another cheap and easy system for the first time self-employed trader who is comfortable with a spreadsheet.

- You still have the work to do of managing the paperwork (checking dates, source and amounts on invoices) and splitting the shares of personal and business expenses.

In the next section we move the technology on to Cloud based bookkeeping where your books are accessible via any Internet connection.

Chapter Eleven – A Free Cloud Based System

Part Three

You mastered the basic idea that bookkeeping is really about using bank and PayPal statements coupled with supporting source evidence to categorise expenses in the first part of this book using a paper and pencil approach of a Simplex style Cash Book. We then moved the technology on to a spreadsheet with its automated additions and expense categorisation using drop down boxes.

In this final section we move the technology on a further step to the use of a dedicated bookkeeping computer package that further automates transaction posting using direct Internet connection to your bank and PayPal accounts' statements

This section of the book will explain and illustrate how to make use of both downloaded bank statement files and also direct Internet links.

With the UK tax based self-employed web trader in mind, the QuickBooks Self-Employed (UK Version) will be examined. This is a subscription based package (£6 a month in 2016, although cheaper offers are sometimes advertised) available via the Appendix link with a free 30 day trial - no credit card details needed.

We are going to explore the QuickBooks Self-Employed web based system. It is a single entry and cash basis accounting system - ideal for the self employed sole trader. It also offers a complete report set out exactly as needed for your tax self assessment needs.

Technology has moved beyond the spreadsheet and its number and text processing abilities now with the advent of web based bookkeeping software applications. These have a much easier to learn, better designed, and intuitive interface with the user, who may find spreadsheets intimidating. You cannot really mess up a bookkeeping computer package structure, but you can mess up a spreadsheet structure easily.

 These bookkeeping packages also take advantage of Internet connections to both access bank and PayPal statement transaction records and to save the books in the 'Cloud' so that the accounts are accessible anywhere there is an Internet connection, and on mobile devices.

You do not have to use QuickBooks Self-Employed. There are alternative free non subscription versions of these type of packages available as well. WAVE is an example that can be found with an Internet search.

Cash Book Automation via an Internet Link to a Bank Account

QuickBooks Self-Employed (QBSE) for the UK user has the attraction of fitting in with the UK 'Simplified Expenses' tax system for sole traders.

The system is designed to IMPORT on line bank statement lines DIRECTLY into the Cash Book. The system uses your normal secure bank current account and PayPal login account name and passwords details over a secure connection.

Manual input of bank statement lines, much like for a spreadsheet, is also possible and easy if you are nervous about connecting your bank account to a new computer program.

You can also just download and save a bank statement file called a CSV file that can be opened in a spreadsheet program for examination prior to importing in to QBSE. You can then switch off your bank account connection and then import the saved CSV file into QuickBooks to give the same effect of all your bank statement lines being added to your list of transactions in one click and then to be able to post transactions to the books once you have verified each item is connected to a matching paper invoice.

The direct net connected and file import CSV file both take in the three bits of familiar key bookkeeping data – the payment or receipt date, the name of the source (or receiver of the funds)and the amount.

The direct bank link, once set up, continues to automatically update your QBSE Cash Book with bank statement lines to check and post to the books whenever you connect to the Internet and log in to your QuickBooks account.

Cloud Systems reduce bookkeeping work.

We once – and maybe still for some people – waited until the end of the month to get a paper bank statement. Then we could do our bank statement checking of our business paperwork to see if the money had actually come in to or gone out of the business.

Technology has changed the way we get information and the timing of getting that information.

So now when we sell an item on eBay, we get an instant notification by email that the money has gone in to our PayPal account and that is OK to send the goods.

We know the business has got the money in – that means we could go ahead and enter the posting into our books. This would also happen if you were paid by bank transfer or paid a cheque in to your account. An on line bank current account can be accessed at any time and payment seen. A cash payment is can be entered into the books as soon as you get it.

With the Simplex Book and the Spreadsheet we started with the monthly bank statement and then WENT BACK and connected our business paperwork – purchase invoices, sales invoices, till receipts and Credit Card and PayPal statements – to the bank statement money movements.

However if we look again at the flow of money in or out chart below we can see that the information for the Cash Book is coming from two directions. One direction is the Invoices and the other direction is the bank statement.

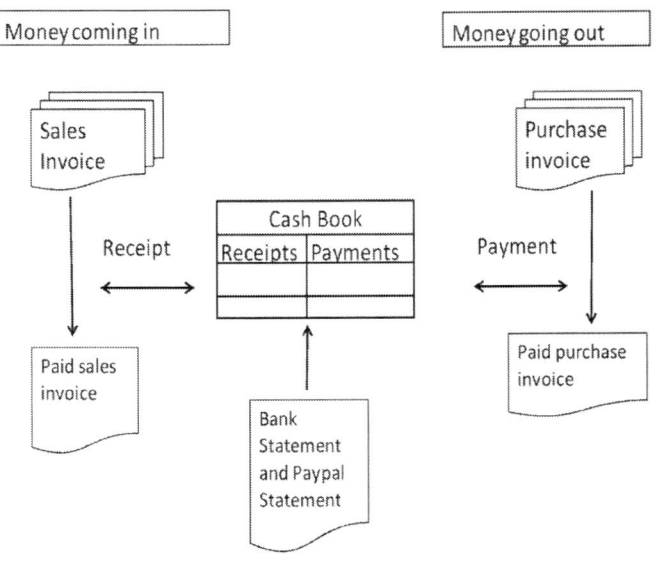

You know that the Cash Book uses a set of entries of the information from the sales or purchase invoices. From invoices we can get the description of the goods or services and the invoice or reference number. These are shown coming down the flow chart.

From the bank statement we get the three key data items- payment date, name and amount. These are the critical three parts of information that the single entry and cash accounting system needs. This is shown coming up the flowchart.

In the QuickBooks Self-Employed method of bookkeeping there will be a coming together of all the information from both directions in one go with several time saving features:

First QBSE can bring in the bank statement data automatically so that whenever you log in to QBSE it links to your bank and imports new transactions for you to check.

 Second QBSE can keep an image or a file copy of the Invoice with its supporting expense category data so you may not need a filing system.

Third QBSE can be set to use a RULE to always treat a particular bank statement entry as a specific expense category. So for example it can treat a bank statement line with a particular supplier name ALWAYS as a Purchase Invoice of for example stationery - saving you time selecting information about expense categories.

To get a feel for how QBSE works we will first examine how QBSE handles a transaction using a manual input of a sales invoice where you type in the Date, Name and Amount yourself. This is rather like using an Analysed Cash Book Spreadsheet. We type in the data from our bank statement and use drop down boxes for income and expense categories.

You can learn as you go along with this explanation by signing up for the QuickBooks Self-Employed free 30 day trial and have a go yourself at these postings. Use the link in the Appendix, get the package and sign in.

QuickBooks Self-Employed - Manual Posting of Transactions

We start by posting a transaction – the sales receipts data manually, where our Gross sales money being paid in records are in our PayPal fees statement. We are manually posting the three key data items of Date, Who From and Amount.

As with the Simplex Cash Book or a spreadsheet Cash Book we only enter the information about a transaction when we know we have been paid. If we are carrying out a manual Sales Invoice entry in QBSE, as with the Simplex Book and the spreadsheet, we rely on a PayPal Fees Activity Statement file export printout which we repeat below to tell us the date the business received the money, who from and the Gross amount.

Date	Time	TimeZ	Name	Type	Status	Curre	Gross	Fee	From	To	Err	Trans
30-04-2	12:45:00	BST	STEPHEN	PayPa	Comp	GBP	60	-2.24	STEVEE29@			4VV66
29-04-2	11:45:00	BST	ALAN AVE	PayPa	Comp	GBP	74.6	-2.34	ALanA	lbrow		8HRD9
28-04-2	21:55:00	BST	PETER AL!	PayPa	Comp	GBP	74.6	-2.34	PandE	lbrow		6BJI12
28-04-2	11:55:00	BST	MATT LEE	PayPa	Comp	GBP	74.6	-2.34	MLEE:	lbrow		5GGI4
28-04-2	20:14:52	BST	Bank Acc(	Withd	Comp	GBP	-560	0				4U810
28-04-2	17:55:00	BST	DAN KNO	PayPa	Comp	GBP	74.6	-2.34	DKNO	lbrow		6SJU3
28-04-2	9:55:00	BST	CARL PEA	PayPa	Comp	GBP	74.6	-2.34	CP123	lbrow		6ugc2
27-04-2	11:55:00	BST	CONNOR	PayPa	Comp	GBP	74.6	-2.34	CCCCr	lbrow		4AGU:
25-04-2	9:17:15	BST	KEITH BAI	PayPa	Comp	GBP	74.6	-2.34	kb123	lbrow		3R050
25-04-2	10:50:45	BST	CARL LYM	PayPa	Comp	GBP	74.6	-2.34	Calrar	lbrow		2CY34
25-04-2	22:52:23	BST	NICHOLA!	PayPa	Comp	GBP	74.6	-2.34	NBB@	lbrow		4CX34
25-04-2	23:55:00	BST	FRANK W	PayPa	Comp	GBP	74.6	-2.34	Frankl	lbrow		3CFY3
24-04-2	9:31:40	BST	ADAM SN	PayPa	Comp	GBP	74.6	-2.34	adam:	lbrow		7MF9:
23-04-2	10:31:40	BST	FRANCES	PayPa	Comp	GBP	74.6	-2.34	fpoole	lbrow		7MF9:
22-04-2	11:31:40	BST	SID JAME:	PayPa	Comp	GBP	74.6	-2.34	sbJam	lbrow		7MF9:
21-04-2	12:31:40	BST	PAUL MIL	PayPa	Comp	GBP	74.6	-2.34	Pjmille	lbrow		7MF9:
20-04-2	13:31:40	BST	SCOTT JO	PayPa	Comp	GBP	74.6	-2.34	scottie	lbrow		7MF9:
19-04-2	14:31:40	BST	LINUS PAI	PayPa	Comp	GBP	74.6	-2.34	lpauli:	lbrow		7MF9:
19-04-2	15:31:40	BST	GERRY RC	PayPa	Comp	GBP	74.6	-2.34	grolan	lbrow		7MF9:
17-04-2	11:55:00	BST	eBay	PayPa	Comp	GBP	-102.05	0				34F32

If you have got the free copy of QuickBooks Self Employed you can copy this next manual posting. After logging in Log, click on the Transactions item on the dark grey left panel. Now click on Add Transaction on the right at the top, under the green Connect Account.

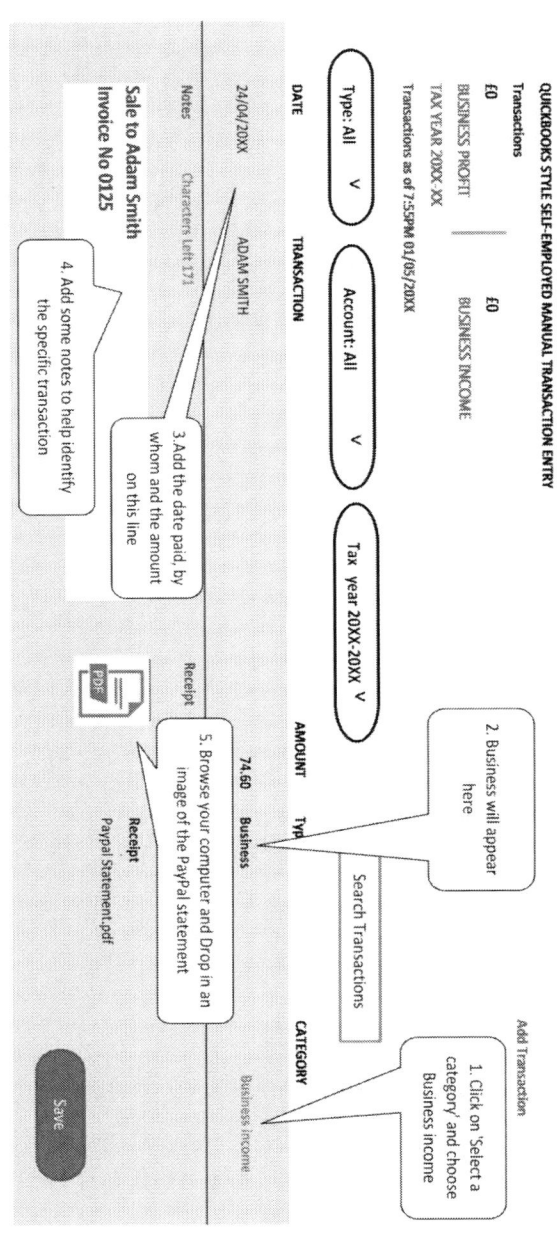

There are some of the usual, plus some extra posting steps (shown in the diagram above and explained below) when using QBSE. After you have signed in and opened the trial software package on your laptop or PC and chosen Transactions from the left hand options and then clicked on Add Transaction, then:

1. Under 'Category' on the right, click on 'Select category' and choose 'Business income'.
2. 'Business will appear under 'Type'
3. Enter the usual date of payment (NOT today's date), whom the income is from and the amount using the PayPal statement details and the GROSS amount.
4. Enter any comments or maybe some product description in the notes box – you will need the associated sales invoice as we did with the Simplex style of Cash Book and spreadsheet postings.
5. You could save a copy of an image of the PayPal statement in the QBSE Cloud account if you have a saved file of it on your computer. Click on 'Browse' and find the file. You would probably continue to file your Sales Invoices paper copies in a Lever Arch File and also save the PayPal account paper copies of statements in a box file, since HMRC need records for 6 years plus the current year.

Now click on the green 'Save' and the transaction has been entered into the books.

If you are interested in using a bank statement direct link to a PayPal or bank account then you can automate much of the data input. We discuss this next.

Sales Invoices – Direct Internet PayPal Account Linking

Technology has now made it possible to directly link your QBSE Cash Book to your PayPal and bank accounts.
However you cannot connect to Louise's bank PayPal account so there is a file you can import in the materials via the Appendix link.

You can use this file when disconnected from an Internet bank or PayPal account. The file is accessed via the link to the kit's training materials via the Appendix. The file is a CSV file that can be opened in a spreadsheet program and also imported into QBSE. But first we show you how to connect directly to a PayPal or bank account and import all the recent transactions (since the last import) with one click.

[Of course you can always try and connect to <u>your own personal</u> PayPal fees account (not this case study) using these instructions below where we explain how Louise will access her PayPal account statement.]

Louise would follow these instructions below to connect DIRECTLY with her own PayPal account to import her money in sales transactions, but it will also import personal payments if she buys using PayPal!

If you are not paid for business goods or services by PayPal you would connect to your shared personal/bank account instead to see the lodgements of cash and cheques in from customers.

Connecting QBSE to your own PayPal fees account

1. Log on to your QuickBooks Self-Employed Trial
2. Click on your name in the right hand corner next to the cog

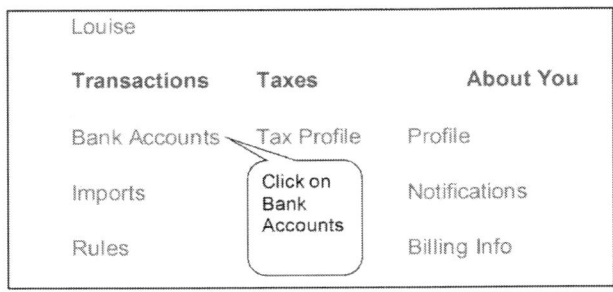

(Note that this table is from a full QuickBooks Self Employed Account and has 'Notifications' and 'Billing' instead of 'Cancel Trial'.)

3.   When the UK banks logos are displayed click on PayPal
4.   When 'Connect your banks and credit cards' page appears click on the PayPal(UK) hyperlink
5.   Log in to your PayPal account with your personal usual email and password
6.   On the permissions page click the Grant Permission button
7.   Back at QuickBooks click on Next
8.   At the message 'Hooray! We successfully downloaded your transactions 1 Account connected' click Done.

9. On the QBSE Homepage click on 'Transactions' on the left hand vertical blue bar

10. You can now treat each direct link imported PayPal fees statement transaction in the same way as the previous section when we entered a manual posting in QBSE.

11. Each sale income will have the gross income and the PayPal fee. Both of these can now be posted to the accounts once you have checked with the Sales Invoice in the usual bookkeeping way.

12. When posting PayPal fees make sure that you choose Business or Personal and then the Category 'Cost of Sales'. You may find that QBSE already thinks that the PayPal fees are bank charges. DO NOT LET THIS HAPPEN - CHOOSE COST OF SALES OR YOU WILL PAY MORE TAX.

13. DO NOT FORGET TO SAVE EACH TRANSACTION by expanding the transaction (little arrow on the right), and then you need to SAVE it – in order to POST it to the Cash Book. You can save an image of the Sales Invoice too.

14. You could add the invoice number to the Notes.

15. Save any Personal PayPal items as Personal.

NOTE:
WHEN POSTING PAYPAL FEES DO NOT LET QBSE CHOOSE BANK CHARGES FOR PAYPAL FEES. INSTEAD CHOOSE 'COST OF SALES FOR RESALE' AS A CATEGORY.

Bank Account Connecting

This direct connecting of the PayPal account works just the same way with your shared Personal/Business bank current account. You will have a lot more personal transactions to mark up as personal and should have only a few business entries – otherwise your bank may want you to have a separate business account. So consider NOT LINKING YOUR bank current account, and just enter any payments manually or you will end up marking and saving a lot of personal items in your books.

Using a PayPal Fees Statement Uploaded File
 If you do not trust linking your PayPal account to your QuickBooks account, then try a file save from your PayPal account instead. Then turn off the bank link and import the file later into QBSE. There is a file with the training materials that you can try out using the instructions below.
 A computer based bookkeeping package such as QuickBooks Self-Employed (QBSE) or the free Wave, has the ability to use an imported file of your PayPal fees statement but it takes a few extra steps. These links are worth it to save time if you have a lot of PayPal items to input.

There is a sort of bug with the CSV PayPal Export.

The PayPal file export saves time but has a slight problem in that when you try and import it into QBSE it uses the NET figure after the PayPal fee. This can be fixed by DELETING the NET COLUMN in the file. Instructions follow below:

Step One - Export the latest bank statement from PayPal. We covered this in the earlier section called PayPal Fees Statement File creation and import.

1. Log in to your PayPal Fees account.
2. Click on the 'Activity' heading to get to that page.
3. Click on the 'Statements' heading in blue on the right of the page near the top.
4. Click on the 'Activity export' choice in the drop down box.
5. At the 'Download History' page the last week is already selected in the Custom Date Range boxes dates - change the dates if you need a wider range.
6. Select the 'File Types for Download' using the drop down box arrow and choose the top one which is 'Comma Delimited - All Activity'.
7. Click on the 'Download History' button.
8. Now DISCONNECT from your bank account.

Step Two - Delete the Imported Net Column of data

1. Look for the file downloading on your computer, make a note where it is, and open the file in a spreadsheet program such as Microsoft Office Excel or Open Office. The file will be called 'Download (XX).csv, where XX is a number.
2. Delete the Net Column (Column 9 around H or J) and save the new file on your computer, where you know where it is. Make sure it stays as a CSV file type and you know what it is called.

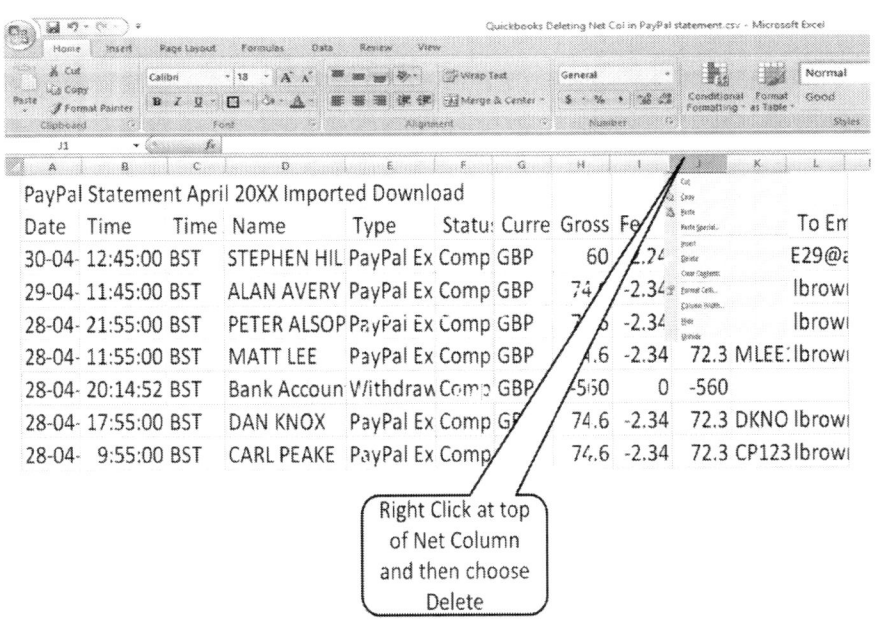

Right Click at top of Net Column and then choose Delete

Having deleted the net column, now right click and save the new file with the deleted column version as a CSV file with a new name

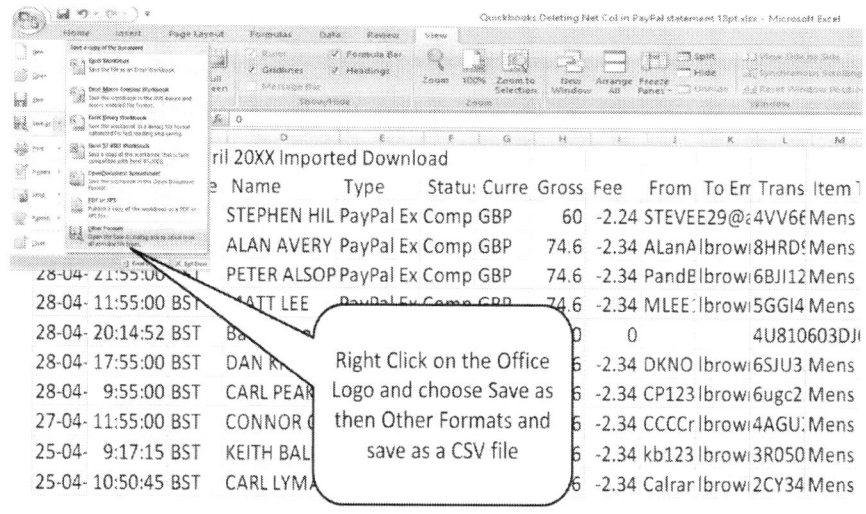

There is a file available via the Appendix link for you to carry out the next steps. This file has the Net column deleted from the CSV file. There is also one without the column deleted for you to try out deleting the Net column.

3. Now log in to your QuickBooks trial and select the cog up in the top right.
4. Click on imports.
5. Click on 'Import older transactions" on the 'Import Transactions' page.
6. Where it says 'how to import' by option 3 – it says 'Locate the CSV file on your computer and upload it here', click 'Browse' and find your file.
7. The file now appears at the bottom of your computer screen 'Import Transactions' page.
8. Now click on the GREEN 'Import' button at the bottom right of the Import Transactions page.
9. When the 'Import Successful' box appears, telling you how many transactions have been imported click 'OK'.
10. You are now back at the 'Import Transaction's page so then to see your imported transactions click on 'Transactions' on the left in the dark blue vertical bar. Once you get to the listed transactions you then work through each one and have the option to select if the amount is Business, Personal or Split. If you have some PayPal transactions that have been imported that are personal, then you should mark each one as such. Otherwise, select Business and the Business Income type in the category box if you are validating a sales invoice line from the PayPal account statement. You will find that the Business/Personal choice box says 'Transfer' until you select business income as a category – then it reverts to Business.

To save the transaction and to add any notes about the customer and a picture of the PayPal payment advice just click on the small arrow at the right of the transaction line under the paper-clip symbol. This will expand the transaction and reveal the SAVE button.

Finally press the GREEN SAVE. That's it!

Import Mistake Fixes

If you find a mistake or that you ended up with the Net figures on one of your imports, you can delete an import. Just return to the Cog at the top of QuickBooks Self-Employed and then click on 'Import older transactions' and then on the 'Import Transactions' page you will find a list of the imported files on the right. Just click on the dustbin and confirm the deletion and have another go at deleting the net column and saving as a CSV file in a spreadsheet program such as Office.

Transaction Mistake Fixes.

Sometimes you mess up a transaction and have saved it. No need to panic. Just select the transaction on the 'Transactions' page and open up the whole picture using the arrow under the staple. Now choose Delete the transaction.

QBSE Summary

This section has concentrated on how you can try out QuickBooks Self-Employed to link to your PayPal and Bank accounts, in order to automate the process of posting transactions.

We can summarise QBSE as having some features compared to the Analysed Spreadsheet Cash Book.

- Adding up automatically saves time and fewer mistakes as there is no transcribing of totals to another page

- Drop down boxes for dates, payment type and expense or income type leads to instant additions in each category and instant analysis of where the money went so far

- There is still no attempt to balance bank account cash with QBSE. With a shared personal/business bank account for a self-employed trader this is not needed anyway

- QBSE reflects the categories of 'Simplified Expenses Tax' system rules for home and car allowances

- QBSE works out your profit as you enter each posting. A real benefit.

- QBSE tells you what your tax and National Insurance will be

- You can import your bank and PayPal statements

- QBSE has an invoice generation, saving and emailing system, but the invoices lack the required UK standard details.

- Another cheap and easy system for the first time self-employed trader who is comfortable with computers and Internet banking security
- As with all bookkeeping there is always some work still to do of managing the paperwork (checking dates, source and amounts on invoices) and splitting the shares of personal and business expenses

Now that you have a good understanding of the books and the income and expenses – the financial accounting - we will go on in this next part to examine what we can learn from all those numbers that we have accumulated. Is our business profitable and, will it stay that way?

Chapter Twelve – Business Cost Structure and Profit

In a sole trader cash basis single entry Cash Book accounting system, the profit (on which income tax and National Insurance is paid) is the difference between the total sales income and the total allowable expenses.

One of the benefits of doing your own books is that you quickly get a feel for the costs and income of the business and do not have to wait until the end of the year for your accountant to tell you if you have made a profit or a loss.

In this next section you are going to learn how to understand the structure of your costs and their relationship to your profits.

In our example of Louise and her eBay business we posted a week of sales and purchases and in that week the sales were about £880 and the Stock, eBay and PayPal fees totalled about £530, with other expenses around £180. So profit looks like £880 less £710 = £110.

But was this a typical week?

Well, there were no costs for Telephone Line Rental since it was paid for a year in advance last month. And we did not have to pay postage on one pair of shoes sold locally.

Unit Costs and Cost Behaviour

To work out if the business will make a profit over a longer period we can examine the unit costs and behaviour of the cost structure.

By unit costs and behaviour of cost structure we mean what makes up the costs and do they vary when we sell more units. Some total costs go up when we sell more. A pair of shoes costs Louise £34.80 from Spanish Shoes. It has a UNIT COST of £34.80. The more Louise sells the more her total cost for buying in shoes goes up. This is called a Variable Cost.

On the other hand she has some costs that are Fixed Costs, at least in the short term. Her eBay 'Basic Business' subscription that allows her 200 listings a month costs £19.99 a month if she sells 10 pairs of shoes or 50 pairs in the month, so it is a fixed cost.

We can use the way the costs behave to find out what the break-even point is for the business. How many shoes must Louise sell to cover her costs and not make a loss or a profit – the break-even point? Once she gets to a break-even point, any extra sales pay her a profit.

Variable Costs

Stock cost is £34.80 per unit.
eBay Commission is £7.46 on a pair (a unit) selling for £74.60.
Postage is £6.60 per unit. These are in the Office costs category.
PayPal Fees at 3% cost £2.34 per unit.
Car Allowance costs at £54 for 37.5 pairs of shoes each month – so the unit cost is £54 divided by 37.5 or £1.44 per unit. Car costs are a variable cost since they only happen when a sale is made.
Stationery – Louise estimates that wrapping paper and other stationery costs are 50p per unit which are also Office Costs.

Total Office costs are then £7.10 per unit.

Total Variable Costs are then £53.14.

The normal selling price is £74.60, so this leaves £74.60 - £53.14 = £21.46 to cover the Fixed Costs. This £21.46 is called the net margin contribution.

Margin contribution is a figure that tells Louise how much profit she will make on every extra pair of shoes that she sells above the break-even point. So if she sold 10 more pairs, above the break-even point she would have a profit of 10 x £21.46 = £214.60. This margin can help a trader to decide if it is worth lowering the selling price to sell more shoes in a quiet period such as in January.

Louise thinks she should be able to sell about 450 pairs of shoes a year or about 37.5 pairs per month on average.

Fixed Costs

The Fixed Costs for a year will be:

eBay Basic Business Subscription £19.99 x 12 = £239.88
Phone Line Rental Business Share = £97.14 see below *
Home use allowance of £10 a month = £120
Broadband and calls package - business share = £12.07 per month x 12 = £144.84

Total Fixed Costs = £601.86

Break-Even Point = Fixed Costs/Margin = £601.86/21.46 = 28 pairs of shoes a year.

So Louise only needs to sell about 2 to 3 pairs a month to recover her fixed costs

Profit on expected annual sales = Margin x Sales Units – Fixed Costs

= £21.46 x 450 = £9657 less Fixed Costs of £601.86

= £9055.14 or about £174 per week.

This will be a good level of 27% return on sales of £33,570 per year. You may think this £15 an hour is a fair return on her 50 hours a month of work in the business. She may have to pay tax on this profit of £9055 if she has other income from her part time job, so the net income will be less than £15 an hour.

Break-even Excel Table

We can make an Excel/Open Office spreadsheet table of the cost structure.

Unit Costs	£
Price	74.60
Number sold	450
Sales Turnover	33,570
Ebay Final Value Fees per unit	7.46
Stock Cost per pair	34.80
Postage and Office Costs	7.10
PayPal Fees	2.34
Car Travel Allowance	1.44
Variable costs per unit	53.14
Unit contribution margin	21.46
Total Gross Margin	9,657
eBay Basic Business Subscription	239.88
Home Use Allowance	120.00
Phone Line Rental Business Share	97.14
Broadband and Calls Business Share	144.84
Total Fixed Costs per period	601.86
Profit = Total Margin less Fixed Costs	9,055
Return on Sales %	27
Annual Breakeven Point (units)	28
Net Profit (Loss)	9,055

A copy of this spreadsheet that you can play with is available via the Appendix link. You can then enter your own business cost structure and play around with changes such as a cost increase or a new sales volume – more or less items sold and see the effect on your profits.

Louise has a profitable business and has a very low level of fixed costs. Most of her costs are variable with stock purchases, eBay, PayPal and postage the main variable costs.

[Note the phone line rental bill is given below with the shared business cost worked out.]

Manipulate the Cost model

Let us examine a change in the competitive environment for Louise. Say the strength of the British pound sterling has dropped by 10% so Louise faces a rise of 10% in the cost of her stock purchases to £38.28 per pair. How will this affect her profits? Here is the new table after the rise in stock costs, assuming that she does not raise her selling prices:

Unit Costs	£
Price	74.60
Number sold	450
Sales Turnover	33,570
Ebay Final Value Fees per unit	7.46
Stock Cost per pair	38.28
Postage and Office Costs	7.10
PayPal Fees	2.34
Car Travel Allowance	1.44
Variable costs per unit	56.62
Unit contribution margin	17.98
Total Gross Margin	8,091
eBay Basic Business Subscription	239.88
Home Use Allowance	120.00
Phone Line Rental Business Share	97.14
Broadband and Calls Business Sha	144.84
Total Fixed Costs per period	601.86
Profit = Total Margin less Fixed Costs	7,489
Return on Sales %	22
Annual Breakeven Point (units)	33

The spreadsheet table shows that Louise has a very high proportion of variable costs, most of which are outside of her control. She will suffer a drop in profit of about £1500 per year if she cannot pass on the rise in her stock costs. However she has very low fixed costs of only £602 per year and so she does not have to sell many pairs of shoes each week to break even. She would want to make a profit to pay her enough for her time she spends on the business work.

The break even spreadsheet table can be manipulated in various ways:

Try a reduction in both the price and also then the eBay Final Value Fees of 10% of the price.
Try a reduction in sales volume of 10%.

You can use the model for your own business costs.

*Phone Line Rental Bill is below:

Your order number is: BTCB0ZZZ123456789
29-Feb-20XX Postcode: ***6DD Thanks

Hello,
Here's an update on your order. Thanks for choosing Line Rental Saver
Because you've paid your line rental in advance, you're not just saving money; you don't need to worry about paying it again for 12 months.
You'll see a refund on your next bill for any monthly or quarterly line rental we've already charged you for the time after you added Line Rental Saver.
At the end of the 12 months, you'll have to pay your line rental every month at the standard price unless you order Line Rental Saver again.
Our prices and terms may change at any time while you're in contract with us
We'll let you know about any important changes before they happen.
Need some help?
Go to bt.com/help

Thanks for choosing us
Barry Libb
Managing Director, Customer Care
The small print
About your terms and conditions
We provide your service under our residential standard terms, our service terms and the tariff guide.
Prices include VAT at 20%. VAT rate and prices are correct at 29-Feb-20XX
You've paid £194.28 by debit card, giving you 10% off our standard price for line rental for a year. You can cancel Line Rental Saver within the first 14 days and get a full refund, but after that it's nonrefundable. There's a 12-month minimum term. Exclusions and conditions apply.

Line Rental per month is £192·28/12 = £16·19
Half for Business = £8·10 per month

We now turn our attention to using our bookkeeping figures for the business to enter the details into a tax return to HMRC for the tax year end for a self employed sole trader.

Chapter Thirteen – Transfer to Tax Return

Part Four

Registration

You will need to tell HMRC about your business before you can complete a self-assessment tax return. You need to register your self employed business with HMRC as soon as you start it, although you will not pay tax until after you get to the end of the tax year.

How to apply for a Government Gateway number and register your business is outside the scope of this book but there is plenty of advice on the HMRC website on how to do this. Go to the link in the Appendix. There is also a link to the HMRC web site where you can submit your tax self-assessment using the figures from your 'books'.

Once registered, eventually you will get to the stage where you need to transfer your bookkeeping summaries of total sales and payments at the end of the year to the on line HMRC self-assessment form. It makes sense to have your company business year in your books start to match the HMRC tax year from April to April. This means that you should start to fill in a Cash Book for the business whenever it starts and then start a new set of Cash Books on the next April 5th. You then complete a tax return for a part tax year to start with, followed by a full tax year at the end of the next year.

If your annual turnover is below the VAT threshold of £82,000 (2016) then you will have the simple task of just entering the total annual sales, the total annual expenses and the net annual profit (or loss.
But for now the three annual figures will be the totals for the part or full tax year, and you will be able to obtain these part tax year, or full tax year annual totals, from the summary pages at the back of your Simplex Cash Book or from the Profit and Loss account in your Analysed Cash Book Spreadsheet.

If you use QuickBooks Self-Employed then there is a useful tax self-assessment report that you can use which we discuss below.

QuickBooks Self-Employed Tax Summary Report

At any time when you are entering postings into QBSE you can click on the grey area on the left on the 'Reports' section to see your tax form report. Then choose 'Tax Summary' and select the year you are interested in from the drop down boxes on the right. Then click 'View'.

At the end of the year, Louise's Tax Summary Report will look like the report below which is a form with expense categories that are based on the HMRC tax form for self employed traders.

QBSE use the layout and box numbers of the 'Full' version of the HMRC form called SA103F where the F is for Full. We can use these figures to fill in the SA103S (Short) version of the tax return.

Profit from business income

QuickBooks Self-Employed Report
Self Assessment Summary
Business Income

Business Income		£			
Your turnover - the takings, fees, sales or money earned by your business		33570	15		
Any other business income not included in box 15		0	16		
TOTAL BUSINESS INCOME		33570			
Business expenses		ALLOWABLE EXPENSES £		DISALLOWABLE EXPENSES £	
Cost of goods bought for resale or goods used		20070	17	£0	32
Construction industry - payments to subcontractors		0	18	£0	33
Wages, salaries and other staff costs		0	19	£0	34
Car, van and travel expenses		648	20	£0	35
Rent, rates, power and insurance costs		120	21	£0	36
Repairs and renewals of property and equipment		0	22	£0	37
Phone, fax, stationery and other office costs		3427	23	£0	38
Advertising and business entertainment costs		240	24	£0	39
Interest on bank and other loans		0	25	£0	40
Bank, credit card and other financial charges		0	26	£0	41
Accountancy, legal and other professional fees		0	28	£0	43
Other business expenses		0	30	£0	45
TOTAL		0	31	£0	46
Net profit or loss					
Total business income		33570		£0	
Total allowable expenses		24505		£0	31
Net Profit		9065		£0	47

Louise only has three items to complete on the short version. After copying the QuickBooks Report data her form then looks like this:

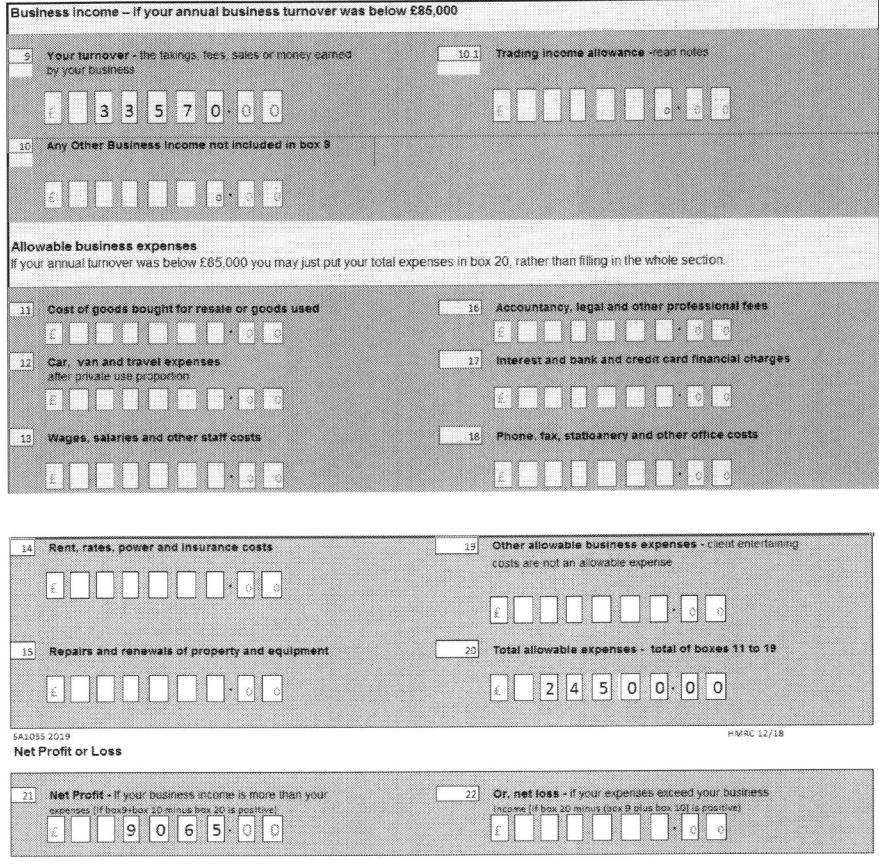

Louise can just fill in the three boxes she needs with her income being below the threshold.

She inputs her total sales, her total allowable expenses and her net profit into the short form.

Income Tax

If Louise had just her self employed business, then with the HMRC tax free allowance (2016/7) of £11,000 (£12500 in 2019/20) she would not pay any income tax on her business profits of £9065 this year.

As it is Louise also earns about £6000 gross from her part time job at Sainsbury's and so her total gross income for income tax purposes is about £15000 a year. She then has a total of £4000 of earnings above the tax free allowance of £11,000 a year (in 2016 and £12,500 in 2019/20) and so she ends up paying about £1000 a year in tax and National Insurance Contributions.

Once you fill in your HMRC on line self assessment and tell HMRC about your other part time income, if any, you will get a tax bill to pay. You are advised to look at the current rates of income tax and National Insurance contributions on the HMRC web site via the Appendix link.

Tax Profile in QBSE - Car and Home Allowances

Allowances for Car/Van and Home Use do not need to be entered into QBSE as transactions. There is a separate entry page accessed on the left hand vertical bar. Then just enter the month's miles and QBSE will use the correct allowance rate in your profit and tax statement report.

Home allowances are set up in your 'Tax Profile' accessed by the cog symbol near your name. You enter the number of hours worked each month and again QBSE adds the correct allowance rate in to your profit and tax report. You may change your hours during the year, so make sure that you put the annual average for the year at the end of the year.

More Taxes – NICs

QBSE works out your taxes for you, including income tax and National Insurance Contributions (NICs) and tells you at the end of the tax report. But if you use the Simplex style forms or spreadsheet you will not know your income tax or NIC amounts due so you will need to consult the latest income and NIC tax rates.

As we have discussed above for Louise, income tax has a tax free allowance of £11,000 (2016 and £12,500 in 2019/20) and income above that is taxed. For any income above the £11,000 there is tax of 20% for the next £21,000 (£37,500 in 2019/20), so an income of £12,000 has £1000 above the tax free allowance and that will incur £200 of tax. There are several web sites that can search for that will calculate your income tax due on any particular income.

You usually pay 2 types of National Insurance if you're self-employed:

Class 2 if your profits and income are £5,965(2016/7 - £6365 in 2019/20) or more a year costs only £2.80 a week (£3 in 2019/20) and is worth it to protect your state pension even with lower profits than £5965 or £6365 in 2019/20.
 Class 4 if your profits and income are £8,060 (£8,632 in 2019/20) or more a year is 9% on profits between £8,060 and £43,000 and 2% on profits over £43,000. (2016/7). The rates are £8,632 and £50,000 in 2019/20.

Planning your tax will help you to keep enough of your profit to pay taxes on time and not incur fines.

Case Study Lessons

Since Louise has a small self employed business and is not registered for VAT her tax affairs are simple. She does not have the complications of accrual accounting and does not have a Limited Company so she uses the HMRC 'Cash Basis' method explained in this book. She has also opted to use the HMRC 'Simplified Expenses' system for allowances used in this book.

Louise can now keep a set of 'books' that she can use to fill in her tax self-assessment form easily with just three year end figures – income, total expenses and profit. She will also have to tell HMRC that she also has other income from her part time job.

She also now has a source document filing system that will meet HMRC needs if they carry out an audit of her business accounts.

She now has a better understanding too about her profits and costs and the effect changes in costs will have on her profits from her break-even table.

****

We hope that you have enjoyed learning how to 'do the books', 'do the filing' and 'do your tax'!

The author welcomes comments and suggestions as to how this book and kit can be improved or extended. Contact him at **rgredfern@hotmail.com**

Chapter Fourteen – Uploading a PayPal Statement

Part Five

Upload a PayPal fees statement

To find out about our PayPal fees charges we need to log on to our on line PayPal account and upload a PayPal fees statement. We need the statement as a source document for the PayPal fees paid for our purchase invoice filing system.

PayPal does not send invoices, but PayPal records its merchant handling fees on each transaction on a statement, which is accessed via the 'Activity' section of the PayPal account web site main page.

In the PayPal Activity section there is a link in the 'Statements' on the right of the web page above Amounts'. See the diagram below. This link accesses a generatable report file, for exporting, of the 'monthly sales report' which has the details of the fees deductions so far in any chosen month.

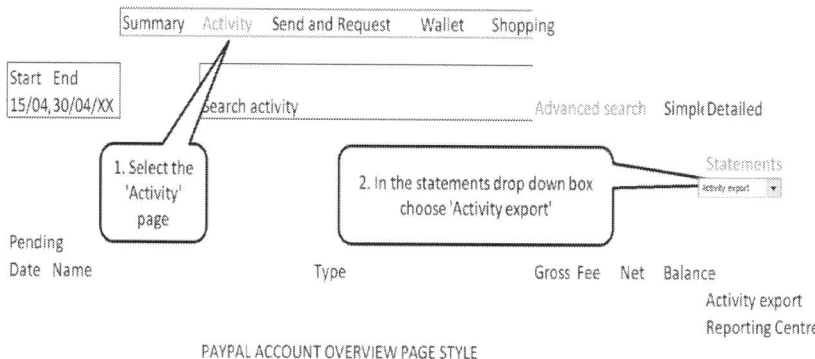

PAYPAL ACCOUNT OVERVIEW PAGE STYLE

Once we get a PayPal fees statement we can deal with bookkeeping and document filing related to the eBay net sales income, PayPal and eBay expense costs.

We will now follow Louise as she deals with her PayPal statement lines in much the same way as dealing with a bank statement.

Louise begins the examination of her PayPal account by exporting the account statement lines for the recent past few weeks.
She first logs on to her PayPal account and selects the 'Activity' page and then clicks on the blue 'Statements' to access the drop down box choice of 'Activity export'. See the diagram above.

In the diagram below, Louise then chooses a set of dates for the second half of April 20XX so she can see the monies in and monies out details. She chooses the Comma Delimited – All Activity, option and then puts in the April dates before finally clicking the 'Download History' button.

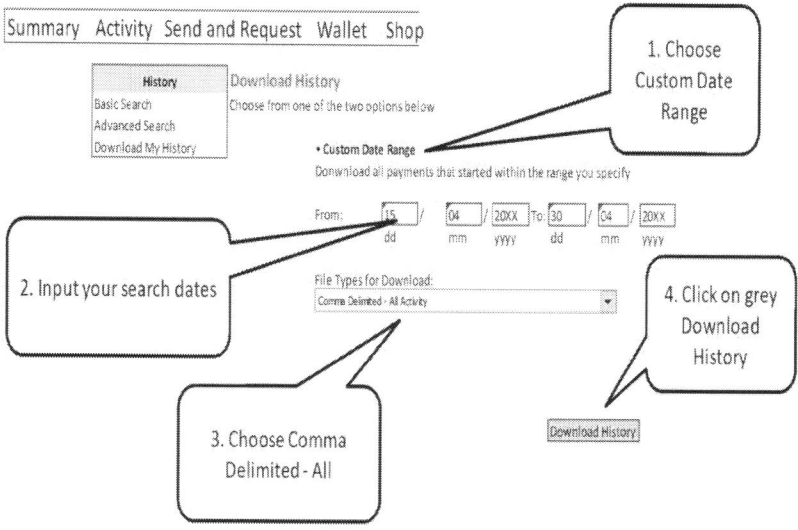

Louise gets the downloaded CSV (1) file which she then opens in her Microsoft Office Excel computer program in order to print out the PayPal fees statement. If she did not have Excel then she could use the free Open Office Spreadsheet program – see the link via the Appendix to get this.

[You might like now to get and print out the PayPal statement and the eBay invoice via the Appendix link so that you can try some bookkeeping postings yourself. You will also need to print out the blank Simplex style Cash Book forms for 'Payments for Business Stock' and 'Payments other than for Stock'.]

The PayPal statement print out for the dates selected is shown below:

Date	Time	Time Z	Name	Type	Statu:	Curre	Gross	Fee	From	To Er	Trans
30-04-2	12:45:00	BST	STEPHEN	PayPa	Comp	GBP	60	-2.24	STEVEE29@ã	4VV6E	
29-04-2	11:45:00	BST	ALAN AVE	PayPa	Comp	GBP	74.6	-2.34	ALanA	brow	8HRD!
28-04-2	21:55:00	BST	PETER AL!	PayPa	Comp	GBP	74.6	-2.34	PandE	brow	6BJI12
28-04-2	11:55:00	BST	MATT LEE	PayPa	Comp	GBP	74.6	-2.34	MLEE:	brow	5GGI4
28-04-2	20:14:52	BST	Bank Acco	Withd	Comp	GBP	-560	0			4U810
28-04-2	17:55:00	BST	DAN KNO	PayPa	Comp	GBP	74.6	-2.34	DKNO	brow	6SJU3
28-04-2	9:55:00	BST	CARL PEA	PayPa	Comp	GBP	74.6	-2.34	CP123	brow	6ugc2
27-04-2	11:55:00	BST	CONNOR	PayPa	Comp	GBP	74.6	-2.34	CCCCr	brow	4AGU:
25-04-2	9:17:15	BST	KEITH BAI	PayPa	Comp	GBP	74.6	-2.34	kb123	brow	3R050
25-04-2	10:50:45	BST	CARL LYM	PayPa	Comp	GBP	74.6	-2.34	Calrar	brow	2CY34
25-04-2	22:52:23	BST	NICHOLA!	PayPa	Comp	GBP	74.6	-2.34	NBB@	brow	4CX34
25-04-2	23:55:00	BST	FRANK W	PayPa	Comp	GBP	74.6	-2.34	Frankl	brow	3CFY3
24-04-2	9:31:40	BST	ADAM SN	PayPa	Comp	GBP	74.6	-2.34	adam:	brow	7MF9:
23-04-2	10:31:40	BST	FRANCES	PayPa	Comp	GBP	74.6	-2.34	fpoole	brow	7MF9:
22-04-2	11:31:40	BST	SID JAME:	PayPa	Comp	GBP	74.6	-2.34	sbJam	brow	7MF9:
21-04-2	12:31:40	BST	PAUL MIL	PayPa	Comp	GBP	74.6	-2.34	Pjmille	brow	7MF9:
20-04-2	13:31:40	BST	SCOTT JO	PayPa	Comp	GBP	74.6	-2.34	scottie	brow	7MF9:
19-04-2	14:31:40	BST	LINUS PAI	PayPa	Comp	GBP	74.6	-2.34	lpauli:	brow	7MF9:
19-04-2	15:31:40	BST	GERRY RC	PayPa	Comp	GBP	74.6	-2.34	grolan	brow	7MF9:
17-04-2	11:55:00	BST	eBay		PayPa	Comp	GBP	-102.05	0		34F32

Chapter Fifteen – Appendix

Study Materials Links to Files to Print Out and Try Out

The best way to try out your own bookkeeping skills as you learn - step by step - how to do your own books, is to print out and use the Case Study business source documents, Simplex style forms and spreadsheets.

Just email the author at rgredfern@hotmail.com for a full set.

- Sales Invoices
- Purchase Invoice
- Till Receipts
- Bank Current Account Statement
- Credit Card Statement
- Simplex style Forms
- Spreadsheet Blank Forms
    Payments
    Sales Invoices
    Receipts
    Profit and Loss
    Statements
- Break Even Spreadsheet

Email the author at rgredfern@hotmail.com for a set of the kit files.

Web Links

Links to QuickBooks, Open Office, etc.:

Open Office Free Spreadsheet program:
https://www.openoffice.org/

HMRC: **www.hmrc.gov.uk**

HMRC: Register for Self Employment:
https://www.gov.uk/set-up-sole-trader/register

HMRC Register for Self Assessment:
https://www.gov.uk/topic/personal-tax/self-assessment

QuickBooks Self-Employed UK Trial Free No Credit Card Needed:
https://selfemployed.intuit.co.uk/login?signup=true&trial=true&promo=tryuk3for6

Pdf reader (Windows):
https://get.adobe.com/uk/reader/
Making Tax Digital :
https://www.gov.uk/government/collections/making-tax-digital-consultations
Please note that the organisations above may change the web addresses, and if so you will need to carry out a Google search for the new web page address.

Study Materials – Larger Pictures

You can get a better view of some of the figures in this book below:

Paperwork

Simplex style Forms

Week No Commencing

Day	Date	Receipts				
		Daily Takings		Other Receipts	Particulars of Other Receipts	Lottery etc Takings
		Cash Col 1	Cheques, Credit & Debit Cards Col 2	Col 3		Col 4
Sub Total					Totals	

Gross Weekly Takings (col 1+2)

Payments for Business Stock

Date or Chq No	To whom paid	Cash Col 9	Cheques, credit and debit cards Col 10

Simplex Style Payments for Business Stock

Simplex Book Page Weekly Layout Style

Payments other than for Stock

Nature of Payment	Cash Col 11	Cheques, credit and debit cards Col 12
Employment Cost (i) Wages		
(ii) Inland Revenue PAYE &NI		
Premises Cost (i) Rent and Rates		
(ii) Light, Heat and Insurance		
(iii) Cleaning		
Repairs		
Gen.Admin. (i) Telephone		
(ii) Postage		
(iii) Stationery, etc.		
Motor Expenses (i) Fuel		
(ii) Servicing & Repairs, etc		
Travel & Subsistence		
Advertising & Entertainment		
Legal and Professional		
Interest Payable		

Statements – Bank, PayPal and Credit card

Bank Statement

Bank Statement April 20XX

Date	Type	Description	Out (£)	In (£)	Balance	
30-04-20XX	DD	CREDIT CARD COMPANY	72.6		1082.53	*Postage paid by credit card*
29-04-20XX	DEB	MARKS&SPENCER PLC CC	60		1155.13	*Groceries*
28-04-20XX	CR	PAYPAL TRANSFER		560	1215.13	*Transfer IN of some of the PayPal balance*
25-04-20XX	DEB	SPANISH SHOES	417.6		655.13	*Purchases of stock*
22-04-20XX	DEB	SAINSBURY'S S/MKT CD !	70.23		1072.73	*Groceries*
22-04-20XX	DEB	SAINSBURYS PETROL CD :	36.95		1142.96	*Petrol BUT – Use car allowance instead*
22-04-20XX	DEB	ALDI CD 5220	13.03		1179.91	*Groceries*
22-04-20XX	DEB	HEATING GAS BOTTLE	30		1192.94	*Heating gas BUT – Use home allowance instead*
22-04-20XX	DD	TESCO MOBILE 12345678	8.7		1222.94	*Groceries*
22-04-20XX	DEB	ASDA PETROL 4415 CD 70	24.76		1231.64	*Petrol BUT – Use car allowance instead*
21-04-20XX	BGC	SAINSBURY A8950		489.15	1256.4	*Sainsburys Pay*
18-04-20XX	DEB	E H BOOTH & CO CD 7025	8.99		767.25	*Groceries*
15-04-20XX	DD	HALIFAX INSURANCE C1:	30		776.24	*Home Insurance BUT – Use home allowance instead*
13-04-20XX	DD	SKY DIGITAL 0022123456:	58.25		806.24	*SKY Subscription*
12-04-20XX	DEB	SAINSBURY'S S/MKT CD !	24.45		864.49	*Groceries*
12-04-20XX	DEB	LIDL UK CD 7025	3.27		888.94	*Groceries*
11-04-20XX	DEB	OCADO RETAIL LIMIT CD	36.09		892.21	*Wine*
11-04-20XX	DEB	DVLA VEHICLE TAX CD 70	145		928.3	*Use car allowance instead*
07-04-20XX	CPT	LNK SPAR - THREE W CD :	50		1073.3	*Cash for personal use*
05-04-20XX	DEB	STATIONERY SUPPLIES	16.54		1123.3	*Printer Paper?*
04-04-20XX	PAY	BANK FEE	5		1139.84	*Bank Fee*
01-04-20XX	DD	BT GROUP PLC MR732783	51.16		1144.84	*Split*
01-04-20XX	SO	OXFAM	4		1196	*Charity donation*

PayPal Statement April 20XX

Date	Time	Time Zone	Name	Type	Status	Currency	Gross	Fee	Net	From Email	To Email
30-04-20XX	12:45:00	BST	STEPHEN HILL	PayPal Exp	Complete	GBP	60	-2.24	57.76	STEVEE29@aol.com	
29-04-20XX	11:45:00	BST	ALAN AVERY	PayPal Exp	Complete	GBP	74.6	-2.34	72.26	AlanAven	lbrown1
28-04-20XX	21:55:00	BST	PETER ALSOP	PayPal Exp	Complete	GBP	74.6	-2.34	72.26	PandBAsl	lbrown1
28-04-20XX	11:55:00	BST	MATT LEE	PayPal Exp	Complete	GBP	74.6	-2.34	72.26	MLEE123@	lbrown1
28-04-20XX	20:14:52	BST	Bank Account	Withdraw	Complete	GBP	-560	0	-560		
28-04-20XX	17:55:00	BST	DAN KNOX	PayPal Exp	Complete	GBP	74.6	-2.34	72.26	DKNOX23	lbrown1
28-04-20XX	9:55:00	BST	CARL PEAKE	PayPal Exp	Complete	GBP	74.6	-2.34	72.26	CP12345@	lbrown1
27-04-20XX	11:55:00	BST	CONNOR COLE	PayPal Exp	Complete	GBP	74.6	-2.34	72.26	CCCCman	lbrown1
25-04-20XX	9:17:15	BST	KEITH BALL	PayPal Exp	Complete	GBP	74.6	-2.34	72.26	Kb1234@c	lbrown1
25-04-20XX	10:50:45	BST	CARL LYMAN	PayPal Exp	Complete	GBP	74.6	-2.34	72.26	Calrand Vl	lbrown1
25-04-20XX	22:52:23	BST	NICHOLAS BUR	PayPal Exp	Complete	GBP	74.6	-2.34	72.26	NBB@hot	lbrown1
25-04-20XX	23:55:00	BST	FRANK WHITE	PayPal Exp	Complete	GBP	74.6	-2.34	72.26	Frankbvh	lbrown1
24-04-20XX	9:31:40	BST	ADAM SMITH	PayPal Exp	Complete	GBP	74.6	-2.34	72.26	adamsmit	lbrown1
23-04-20XX	10:31:40	BST	FRANCES POOL	PayPal Exp	Complete	GBP	74.6	-2.34	72.26	fpoole 12	lbrown1
22-04-20XX	11:31:40	BST	SID JAMESON	PayPal Exp	Complete	GBP	74.6	-2.34	72.26	sbJames2	lbrown1
21-04-20XX	12:31:40	BST	PAUL MILLER	PayPal Exp	Complete	GBP	74.6	-2.34	72.26	Pjmiller@	lbrown1
20-04-20XX	13:31:40	BST	SCOTT JOHANN	PayPal Exp	Complete	GBP	74.6	-2.34	72.26	scottiedo	lbrown1
19-04-20XX	14:31:40	BST	LINUS PAULIS	PayPal Exp	Complete	GBP	74.6	-2.34	72.26	lpaulis109	lbrown1
19-04-20XX	15:31:40	BST	GERRY ROLAND	PayPal Exp	Complete	GBP	74.6	-2.34	72.26	groland92	lbrown1
17-04-20XX	11:55:00	BST	eBay	PayPal Exp	Complete	GBP	-102.05	0	-102.05		

PayPal Statement

Credit Card Statement

Transaction Date	Posting Date	Billing Am	Merchant	Merchant	Merchant	Merchant Reference Nu	Debit	SICMCC Code
30-04-20XX	30-04-20XX	£72.60	DIRECT DEBIT P	THANK YOU			C	0
29-04-20XX	29-04-20XX	£6.60	POST OFF	WIRRAL	GBR	CH49 3NQ	5.53778E+22 D	5542
29-04-20XX	29-04-20XX	£6.60	POST OFF	WIRRAL	GBR	CH49 3NQ	5.53778E+22 D	5542
28-04-20XX	28-04-20XX	£6.60	POST OFF	WIRRAL	GBR	CH49 3NQ	5.53778E+22 D	5542
28-04-20XX	28-04-20XX	£6.60	POST OFF	WIRRAL	GBR	CH49 3NQ	5.53778E+22 D	5542
28-04-20XX	28-04-20XX	£6.60	POST OFF	WIRRAL	GBR	CH49 3NQ	5.53778E+22 D	5542
27-04-20XX	27-04-20XX	£6.60	POST OFF	WIRRAL	GBR	CH49 3NQ	5.53778E+22 D	5542
25-04-20XX	25-04-20XX	£6.60	POST OFF	WIRRAL	GBR	CH49 3NQ	5.53778E+22 D	5542
25-04-20XX	25-04-20XX	£6.60	POST OFF	WIRRAL	GBR	CH49 3NQ	5.53778E+22 D	5542
25-04-20XX	25-04-20XX	£6.60	POST OFF	WIRRAL	GBR	CH49 3NQ	5.53778E+22 D	5542
25-04-20XX	25-04-20XX	£6.60	POST OFF	WIRRAL	GBR	CH49 3NQ	5.53778E+22 D	5542
24-04-20XX	24-04-20XX	£6.60	POST OFF	WIRRAL	GBR	CH49 3NQ	5.53778E+22 D	5542

Credit Card Statement

3. Invoices and Bills – Examples (for the full set get the files from the author by email):

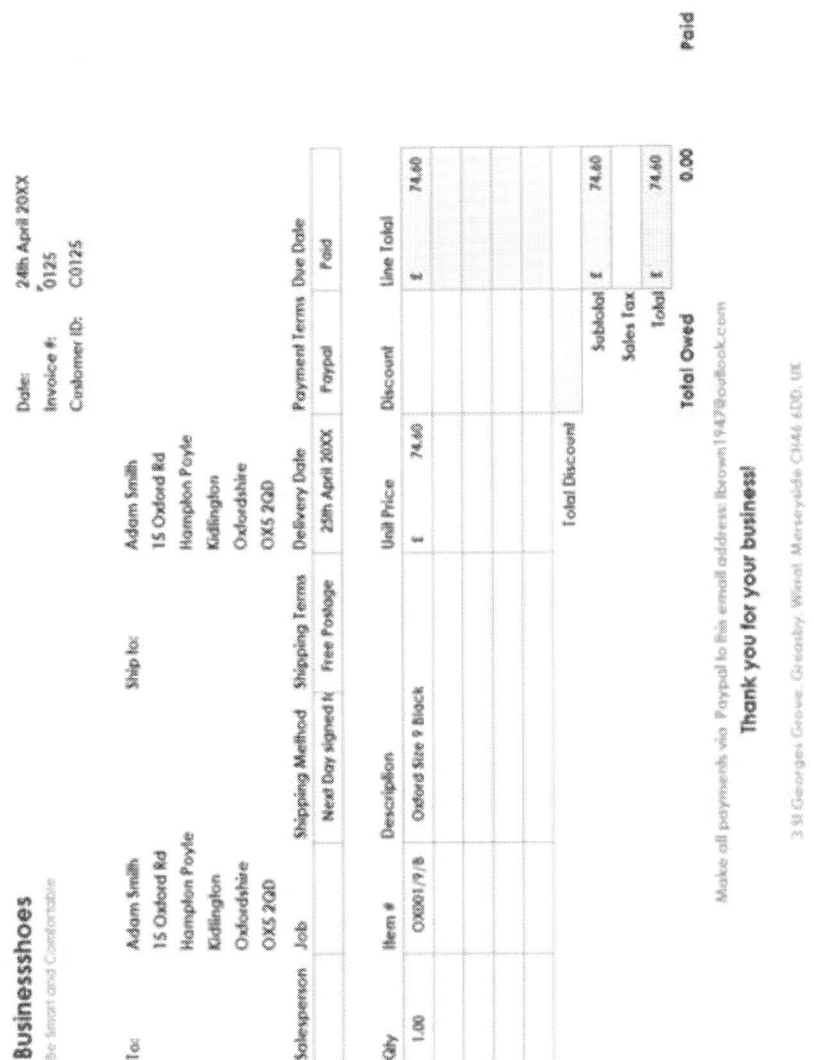

Sales Invoice

Purchase Invoice

Spanish Shoes

Invoice To:
Mrs. L. Brown
Businessshoes
3 St Georges
Greasby
Wirral
Merseyside
CH46 6DD
UK
0151623405
03261

Delivery Address:
Mrs. L. Brown
Businessshoes
3 St Georges Grove
Greasby
Wirral
Merseyside
CH46 6DD
UK
Phone 0151623405
Customer ID 03261

Date: 25/04/20XX
Customer #: 7804
Invoice #: 0420
Terms: Cash Account

Invoice

Qty	Item No	Description	Unit Price £	Total £
4	P14001/09	Mens Derby Lace Up Black Size 9	29.00	116.00
4	P12001/10	Mens Oxford Lace Up Black Size 10	29.00	116.00
4	P14001/11	Mens Derby Lace Up Black Size 11	29.00	116.00
			Subtotal	348.00
			VAT	69.60
			Total £	417.60

Make all cheques payable to Spanishshoes

Thank you for your business!

Post Ofice Lt.
Your Receipt

140 Greasby Rd
Wirral
CH49 3NQ

Date and Time	24/04/20XX 12:15
Session ID:	2-555136
Dest	UK (EU)
Quantity	1
Weight	1.5 Kg
1st Class Packet	£6.60
Total Cost of Services	£6.60

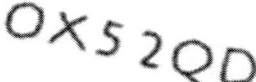

OX5 2QD

IT IS IMPORTANT THAT YOU RETAIN THIS
RECEIPT AS IT IS PROOF OF YOUR POSTING

PLEASE REFER TO SEPARATE TERMS AND CONDITIONS

For information regarding
Mail
products and services
contact us on
08456 740 740
or visit our website at
www.postofice.co.uk

Post Office Till Receipt

Stationery Supplies

Billing Address	Shipping Address
Mrs. L. Brown	Mrs. L. Brown
3 St Georges Grove	3 St Georges Grove
Greasby	Greasby
Wirral	Wirral
Merseyside	Merseyside
CH46 6DD	CH46 6DD

Invoice for

Your order of 05 April, 20XX   Order ID 202-0661-704-3052340   Invoice number DYTMSDRGb

Invoice Date 05 April 20XX

Qty	Item	Bin	Our Price (excl.VAT)	VAT Rate	Total Price
1	5 Star Office Value Copier Paper Ream Wrapped 75gsm A4 White	(**p-1-82508860)**	£13.78	20%	£16.54
	Shipping Charges		£0.00		£0.00

Subtotal (excl VAT)	Subtot (excl VAT)	VAT at	Total VAT		Total
0%	20%	20%			
£0.00	£13.78	£2.76	£2.76		£16.54

Conversion Rate £1.00 : EUR 1.17

This shipment completes your order which has been paid.

Balance to Pay £0.00

Stationery Purchase Invoice

Telephone and Broadband Rental and other charges

Phone line – 0151623405
Line Rental

05 May - 04 Jun 201XX

£0.00

Because you've got Line Rental Saver your line rental is paid until
28 Mar 20XX

Package
Broadband and Calls

05 May – 04 Jun 20XX. This is the cost of your Package at £21.80 a month, charged in advance

from 05 May – 04 Jun 20XX. This gives you:

- **Calling Plan** Unlimited Evening and Weekend Plan
- **Broadband** Unlimited Broadband

£21.80

Sport
Sport Pack

05 May – 04 Jun 20XX. This is the cost of your Sport on the Digital Satellite Platform at
£5.00 a month, charged in advance from 05 May 20XX to 04 Jun 20XX

£5.00

Sport HD Pack
05 May – 04 Jun 20XX. This is the cost of your Sport HD Pack at £4.00 a month, charged in
advance from 05 May 20XX to 04 Jun 20XX

£4.00

Mobile
Mobile 500MB Plan 01234 5678910

05 May - 04 Jun 20XX. This is the cost of your mobile plan at £10.00, charged in advance
from 05 May - 04 Jun 20XX

£10.00

Broadband Discount 0151623405

05 May - 04 Jun 16
Because you have our broadband your mobile bill is less

-£5.00

Total rental and other charges

£35.80

Phone usage for 0151623405

You made 18 call(s) - number of free call(s)s.

£15.23

Mobile usage for 01234 5678910

£0.14

Charges not covered by your mobile plan.
0 minutes, 8 messages, 0MB data

Total usage charges

£15.36

Total including any applicable taxes   £51.16

Telephone Bill Parts 1 to 3

Your order number is:
CB0322123456789
29-Feb-20XX

Postcode: ****6DD

Thanks

Hello,

Here's an update on your order.

Thanks for choosing Line Rental Saver

Because you've paid your line rental in advance, you're not just saving money, you don't need to worry about paying it again for 12 months.

You'll see a refund on your next bill for any monthly or quarterly line rental we've already charged you for the time after you added Line Rental Saver.

At the end of the 12 months, you'll have to pay your line rental every month at the standard price unless you order Line Rental Saver again.

Need some help?

Go to bt.com/help

Thanks for choosing us

Barry Libb
Managing Director, Customer Care

The small print

About your terms and conditions
We provide your service under our residential standard terms, our service terms and the tariff guide.

Prices include VAT at 20%. VAT rate and prices are correct at 29-Feb-20XX

You've paid £194.28 by debit card, giving you 10% off our standard price for line rental for a year. You can cancel Line Rental Saver within the first 14 days and get a full refund, but after that it's non-refundable. There's a 12-month minimum term. Exclusions and conditions apply.

Line Rental per month is £194.28/12 = 16.19—
half for business = £8.10 per month

Telephone Line Rental Bill

Sole Trader Tax Form – Top Part

Business income – if your annual business turnover was below £85,000

9 **Your turnover** - the takings, fees, sales or money earned by your business

£ 3 3 5 7 0 · 0 0

10 Any Other Business income not included in box 9

£ 0 · 0 0

10.1 **Trading income allowance** –read notes

£ 0 · 0 0

Allowable business expenses
If your annual turnover was below £85,000 you may just put your total expenses in box 20, rather than filling in the whole section.

11 **Cost of goods bought for resale or goods used**

£ 0 · 0 0

12 **Car, van and travel expenses** after private use proportion

£ 0 · 0 0

13 **Wages, salaries and other staff costs**

16 **Accountancy, legal and other professional fees**

£ 0 · 0 0

17 **Interest and bank and credit card financial charges**

£ 0 · 0 0

18 **Phone, fax, stationery and other office costs**

Sole Trader Tax Form last part

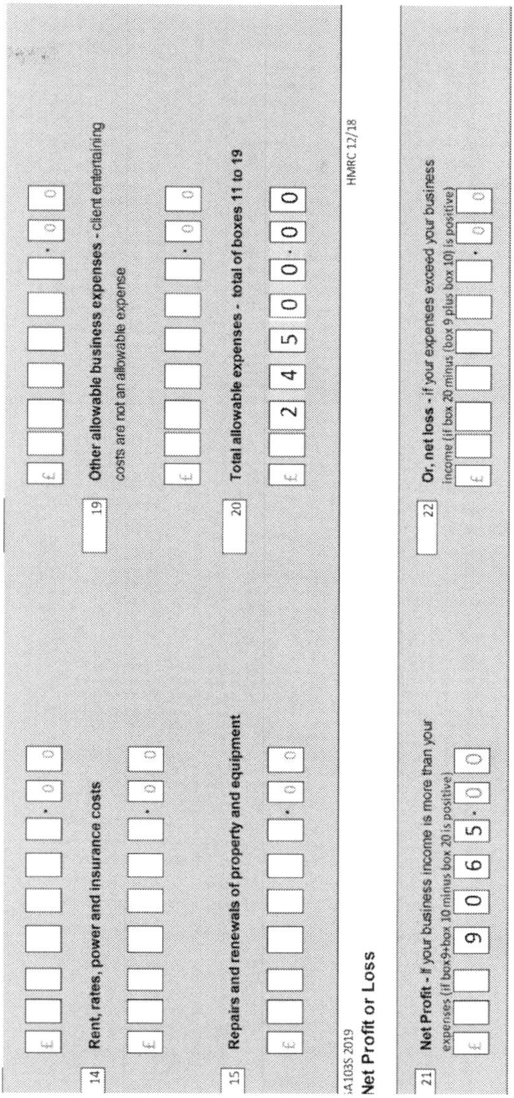

14 Rent, rates, power and insurance costs

£ . 0 0

15 Repairs and renewals of property and equipment

£ . 0 0

19 Other allowable business expenses - client entertaining costs are not an allowable expense

£ . 0 0

20 Total allowable expenses - total of boxes 11 to 19

£ 2450.00

SA103S 2019

HMRC 12/18

Net Profit or Loss

21 Net Profit - if your business income is more than your expenses (if box9+box 10 minus box 20 is positive)

£ 9065.00

22 Or, net loss - if your expenses exceed your business income (if box 20 minus (box 9 plus box 10) is positive)

£ . 0 0

Printed in Great Britain
by Amazon